Lord Weary's Castle

AND

The Mills of the Kavanaughs

Lord Weary's Castle

and

The Mills of the Kavanaughs

by

Robert Lowell

HBJ

A Harvest/HBJ Book
Harcourt Brace Jovanovich, Publishers
San Diego   New York   London

Printed in the United States of America

Library of Congress Cataloging in Publication Data
Lowell, Robert, 1917–1977.
Lord Weary's castle; and, The mills of the Kavanaughs.
(A Harvest/HBJ book)
I. Lowell, Robert, 1917–1977. Mills of the Kavanaughs.
1983. II. Title.
PS3523.089A6   1983   811'.52   83-8468
ISBN 0-15-653500-9

A B C D E F G H I J

Library of Congress Catalog Card Number: 61-8124

Contents

Lord Weary's Castle

The Mills of the Kavanaughs

Lord Weary's Castle

To Jean

Some of these poems have appeared in *Partisan Review*, *The Sewanee Review*, *The Kenyon Review*, *The Nation*, *Common Sense*, *Portfolio*, *Foreground*, *The Commonweal*, *Poetry*, *The Virginia Quarterly*, and in "Land of Unlikeness," published by the Cummington Press.

Note

My title comes from an old ballad:

> "It's Lambkin was a mason good
> As ever built wi' stane:
> He built Lord Wearie's castle
> But payment gat he nane . . ."

When I use the word *after* below the title of a poem, what follows is not a translation but an imitation which should be read as though it were an original English poem. The last line of "The Shako" is taken literally from a translation by C. F. McIntyre. "Our Lady of Walsingham" is an adaptation of several paragraphs from E. I. Watkin's *Catholic Art and Culture*. I hope that the source of "After the Surprising Conversions" will be recognized.

R. L.

Suscipe, Domine, munera pro tuorum commemoratione Sanctorum: ut, sicut illos passio gloriosos effecit; ita nos devotio reddat innocuos.

The Exile's Return

THERE mounts in squalls a sort of rusty mire,
Not ice, not snow, to leaguer the Hôtel
De Ville, where braced pig-iron dragons grip
The blizzard to their rigor mortis. A bell
Grumbles when the reverberations strip
The thatching from its spire,
The search-guns click and spit and split up timber
And nick the slate roofs on the Holstenwall
Where torn-up tilestones crown the victor. Fall
And winter, spring and summer, guns unlimber
And lumber down the narrow gabled street
Past your gray, sorry and ancestral house
Where the dynamited walnut tree
Shadows a squat, old, wind-torn gate and cows
The Yankee commandant. You will not see
Strutting children or meet
The peg-leg and reproachful chancellor
With a forget-me-not in his button-hole
When the unseasoned liberators roll
Into the Market Square, ground arms before
The Rathaus; but already lily-stands
Burgeon the risen Rhineland, and a rough
Cathedral lifts its eye. Pleasant enough,
Voi ch'entrate, and your life is in your hands.

The Holy Innocents

LISTEN, the hay-bells tinkle as the cart
Wavers on rubber tires along the tar
And cindered ice below the burlap mill
And ale-wife run. The oxen drool and start
In wonder at the fenders of a car,
And blunder hugely up St. Peter's hill.
These are the undefiled by woman—their
Sorrow is not the sorrow of this world:
King Herod shrieking vengeance at the curled
Up knees of Jesus choking in the air,

A king of speechless clods and infants. Still
The world out-Herods Herod; and the year,
The nineteen-hundred forty-fifth of grace,
Lumbers with losses up the clinkered hill
Of our purgation; and the oxen near
The worn foundations of their resting-place,
The holy manger where their bed is corn
And holly torn for Christmas. If they die,
As Jesus, in the harness, who will mourn?
Lamb of the shepherds, Child, how still you lie.

Colloquy in Black Rock

Here the jack-hammer jabs into the ocean;
My heart, you race and stagger and demand
More blood-gangs for your nigger-brass percussions,
Till I, the stunned machine of your devotion,
Clanging upon this cymbal of a hand,
Am rattled screw and footloose. All discussions

End in the mud-flat detritus of death.
My heart, beat faster, faster. In Black Mud
Hungarian workmen give their blood
For the martyre Stephen, who was stoned to death.

Black Mud, a name to conjure with: O mud
For watermelons gutted to the crust,
Mud for the mole-tide harbor, mud for mouse,
Mud for the armored Diesel fishing tubs that thud
A year and a day to wind and tide; the dust
Is on this skipping heart that shakes my house,

House of our Savior who was hanged till death.
My heart, beat faster, faster. In Black Mud
Stephen the martyre was broken down to blood:
Our ransom is the rubble of his death.

Christ walks on the black water. In Black Mud
Darts the kingfisher. On Corpus Christi, heart,
Over the drum-beat of St. Stephen's choir
I hear him, *Stupor Mundi,* and the mud
Flies from his hunching wings and beak—my heart,
The blue kingfisher dives on you in fire.

Christmas in Black Rock

CHRIST God's red shadow hangs upon the wall
The dead leaf's echo on these hours
Whose burden spindles to no breath at all;
Hard at our heels the huntress moonlight towers
And the green needles bristle at the glass
Tiers of defense-plants where the treadmill night
Churns up Long Island Sound with piston-fist.
Tonight, my child, the lifeless leaves will mass,
Heaving and heaping, as the swivelled light
Burns on the bell-spar in the fruitless mist.

Christ Child, your lips are lean and evergreen
Tonight in Black Rock, and the moon
Sidles outside into the needle-screen
And strikes the hand that feeds you with a spoon
Tonight, as drunken Polish night-shifts walk
Over the causeway and their juke-box booms
Hosannah in excelsis Domino.
Tonight, my child, the foot-loose hallows stalk
Us down in the blind alleys of our rooms;
By the mined root the leaves will overflow.

December, old leech, has leafed through Autumn's store
Where Poland has unleashed its dogs
To bay the moon upon the Black Rock shore:
Under our windows, on the rotten logs
The moonbeam, bobbing like an apple, snags
The undertow. O Christ, the spiralling years
Slither with child and manger to a ball
Of ice; and what is man? We tear our rags
To hang the Furies by their itching ears,
And the green needles nail us to the wall.

New Year's Day

Again and then again . . . the year is born
To ice and death, and it will never do
To skulk behind storm-windows by the stove
To hear the postgirl sounding her French horn
When the thin tidal ice is wearing through.
Here is the understanding not to love
Our neighbor, or tomorrow that will sieve
Our resolutions. While we live, we live

To snuff the smoke of victims. In the snow
The kitten heaved its hindlegs, as if fouled,
And died. We bent it in a Christmas box
And scattered blazing weeds to scare the crow
Until the snake-tailed sea-winds coughed and howled
For alms outside the church whose double locks
Wait for St. Peter, the distorted key.
Under St. Peter's bell the parish sea

Swells with its smelt into the burlap shack
Where Joseph plucks his hand-lines like a harp,
And hears the fearful *Puer natus est*
Of Circumcision, and relives the wrack
And howls of Jesus whom he holds. How sharp
The burden of the Law before the beast:
Time and the grindstone and the knife of God.
The Child is born in blood, O child of blood.

The Quaker Graveyard in Nantucket

(FOR WARREN WINSLOW, DEAD AT SEA)

Let man have dominion over the fishes of the sea and the
fowls of the air and the beasts and the whole earth, and
every creeping creature that moveth upon the earth.

I

A BRACKISH reach of shoal off Madaket,—
The sea was still breaking violently and night
Had steamed into our North Atlantic Fleet,
When the drowned sailor clutched the drag-net. Light
Flashed from his matted head and marble feet,
He grappled at the net
With the coiled, hurdling muscles of his thighs:
The corpse was bloodless, a botch of reds and whites,
Its open, staring eyes
Were lustreless dead-lights
Or cabin-windows on a stranded hulk
Heavy with sand. We weight the body, close
Its eyes and heave it seaward whence it came,
Where the heel-headed dogfish barks its nose
On Ahab's void and forehead; and the name
Is blocked in yellow chalk.
Sailors, who pitch this portent at the sea
Where dreadnaughts shall confess
Its hell-bent deity,
When you are powerless
To sand-bag this Atlantic bulwark, faced
By the earth-shaker, green, unwearied, chaste
In his steel scales: ask for no Orphean lute
To pluck life back. The guns of the steeled fleet
Recoil and then repeat
The hoarse salute.

WHENEVER winds are moving and their breath
Heaves at the roped-in bulwarks of this pier,
The terns and sea-gulls tremble at your death
In these home waters. Sailor, can you hear
The Pequod's sea wings, beating landward, fall
Headlong and break on our Atlantic wall
Off 'Sconset, where the yawing S-boats splash
The bellbuoy, with ballooning spinnakers,
As the entangled, screeching mainsheet clears
The blocks: off Madaket, where lubbers lash
The heavy surf and throw their long lead squids
For blue-fish? Sea-gulls blink their heavy lids
Seaward. The winds' wings beat upon the stones,
Cousin, and scream for you and the claws rush
At the sea's throat and wring it in the slush
Of this old Quaker graveyard where the bones
Cry out in the long night for the hurt beast
Bobbing by Ahab's whaleboats in the East.

ALL YOU recovered from Poseidon died
With you, my cousin, and the harrowed brine
Is fruitless on the blue beard of the god,
Stretching beyond us to the castles in Spain,
Nantucket's westward haven. To Cape Cod
Guns, cradled on the tide,
Blast the eelgrass about a waterclock
Of bilge and backwash, roil the salt and sand
Lashing earth's scaffold, rock
Our warships in the hand
Of the great God, where time's contrition blues
Whatever it was these Quaker sailors lost
In the mad scramble of their lives. They died
When time was open-eyed,
Wooden and childish; only bones abide
There, in the nowhere, where their boats were tossed
Sky-high, where mariners had fabled news
Of IS, the whited monster. What it cost
Them is their secret. In the sperm-whale's slick
I see the Quakers drown and hear their cry:
"If God himself had not been on our side,
If God himself had not been on our side,
When the Atlantic rose against us, why,
Then it had swallowed us up quick."

IV

THIS is the end of the whaleroad and the whale
Who spewed Nantucket bones on the thrashed swell
And stirred the troubled waters to whirlpools
To send the Pequod packing off to hell:
This is the end of them, three-quarters fools,
Snatching at straws to sail
Seaward and seaward on the turntail whale,
Spouting out blood and water as it rolls,
Sick as a dog to these Atlantic shoals:
Clamavimus, O depths. Let the sea-gulls wail

For water, for the deep where the high tide
Mutters to its hurt self, mutters and ebbs.
Waves wallow in their wash, go out and out,
Leave only the death-rattle of the crabs,
The beach increasing, its enormous snout
Sucking the ocean's side.
This is the end of running on the waves;
We are poured out like water. Who will dance
The mast-lashed master of Leviathans
Up from this field of Quakers in their unstoned graves?

WHEN the whale's viscera go and the roll
Of its corruption overruns this world
Beyond tree-swept Nantucket and Wood's Hole
And Martha's Vineyard, Sailor, will your sword
Whistle and fall and sink into the fat?
In the great ash-pit of Jehoshaphat
The bones cry for the blood of the white whale,
The fat flukes arch and whack about its ears,
The death-lance churns into the sanctuary, tears
The gun-blue swingle, heaving like a flail,
And hacks the coiling life out: it works and drags
And rips the sperm-whale's midriff into rags,
Gobbets of blubber spill to wind and weather,
Sailor, and gulls go round the stoven timbers
Where the morning stars sing out together
And thunder shakes the white surf and dismembers
The red flag hammered in the mast-head. Hide,
Our steel, Jonas Messias, in Thy side.

OUR LADY OF WALSINGHAM

THERE once the penitents took off their shoes
And then walked barefoot the remaining mile;
And the small trees, a stream and hedgerows file
Slowly along the munching English lane,
Like cows to the old shrine, until you lose
Track of your dragging pain.
The stream flows down under the druid tree,
Shiloah's whirlpools gurgle and make glad
The castle of God. Sailor, you were glad
And whistled Sion by that stream. But see:

Our Lady, too small for her canopy,
Sits near the altar. There's no comeliness
At all or charm in that expressionless
Face with its heavy eyelids. As before,
This face, for centuries a memory,
Non est species, neque decor,
Expressionless, expresses God: it goes
Past castled Sion. She knows what God knows,
Not Calvary's Cross nor crib at Bethlehem
Now, and the world shall come to Walsingham.

VII

THE EMPTY winds are creaking and the oak
Splatters and splatters on the cenotaph,
The boughs are trembling and a gaff
Bobs on the untimely stroke
Of the greased wash exploding on a shoal-bell
In the old mouth of the Atlantic. It's well;
Atlantic, you are fouled with the blue sailors,
Sea-monsters, upward angel, downward fish:
Unmarried and corroding, spare of flesh
Mart once of supercilious, wing'd clippers,
Atlantic, where your bell-trap guts its spoil
You could cut the brackish winds with a knife
Here in Nantucket, and cast up the time
When the Lord God formed man from the sea's slime
And breathed into his face the breath of life,
And blue-lung'd combers lumbered to the kill.
The Lord survives the rainbow of His will.

The First Sunday in Lent

I

IN THE ATTIC

The crooked family chestnut sighs, for March,
Time's fool, is storming up and down the town;
The gray snow squelches and the well-born stamp
From sermons in a scolded, sober mob
That wears away the Sabbath with a frown,
A world below my window. What will clamp
The weak-kneed roots together when the damp
Aches like a conscience, and they grope to rob
The hero under his triumphal arch?

This is the fifth floor attic where I hid
My stolen agates and the cannister
Preserved from Bunker Hill—feathers and guns,
Matchlock and flintlock and percussion-cap;
Gettysburg etched upon the cylinder
Of Father's Colt. A Lüger of a Hun,
Once blue as Satan, breaks Napoleon,
My china pitcher. Cartridge boxes trap
A chipmunk on the saber where they slid.

On Troy's last day, alas, the populous
Shrines held carnival, and girls and boys
Flung garlands to the wooden horse; so we
Burrow into the lion's mouth to die.
Lord, from the lust and dust thy will destroys
Raise an unblemished Adam who will see
The limbs of the tormented chestnut tree
Tingle, and hear the March-winds lift and cry:
"The Lord of Hosts will overshadow us."

THE FERRIS WHEEL

THIS world, this ferris wheel, is tired and strains
Its townsman's humorous and bulging eye,
As he ascends and lurches from his seat
And dangles by a shoe-string overhead
To tell the racing world that it must die.
Who can remember what his father said?
The little wheel is turning on the great
In the white water of Christ's blood. The red
Eagle of Ares swings along the lanes,

Of camp-stools where the many watch the sky:
The townsman hangs, the eagle swings. It stoops
And lifts the ferris wheel into the tent
Pitched for the devil. But the man works loose,
He drags and zigzags through the circus hoops,
And lion-taming Satan bows and loops
His cracking tail into a hangman's noose;
He is the only happy man in Lent.
He laughs into my face until I cry.

Christmas Eve Under Hooker's Statue

Tonight a blackout. Twenty years ago
I hung my stocking on the tree, and hell's
Serpent entwined the apple in the toe
To sting the child with knowledge. Hooker's heels
Kicking at nothing in the shifting snow,
A cannon and a cairn of cannon balls
Rusting before the blackened Statehouse, know
How the long horn of plenty broke like glass
In Hooker's gauntlets. Once I came from Mass;

Now storm-clouds shelter Christmas, once again
Mars meets his fruitless star with open arms,
His heavy saber flashes with the rime,
The war-god's bronzed and empty forehead forms
Anonymous machinery from raw men;
The cannon on the Common cannot stun
The blundering butcher as he rides on Time—
The barrel clinks with holly. I am cold:
I ask for bread, my father gives me mould;

His stocking is full of stones. Santa in red
Is crowned with wizened berries. Man of war,
Where is the summer's garden? In its bed
The ancient speckled serpent will appear,
And black-eyed susan with her frizzled head.
When Chancellorsville mowed down the volunteer,
"All wars are boyish," Herman Melville said;
But we are old, our fields are running wild:
Till Christ again turn wanderer and child.

Buttercups

WHEN we were children our papas were stout
And colorless as seaweed or the floats
At anchor off New Bedford. We were shut
In gardens where our brassy sailor coats
Made us like black-eyed susans bending out
Into the ocean. Then my teeth were cut:
A levelled broom-pole butt
Was pushed into my thin
And up-turned chin—
There were shod hoofs behind the horseplay. But
I played Napoleon in my attic cell
Until my shouldered broom
Bobbed down the room
With horse and neighing shell.

Recall the shadows the doll-curtains veined
On Ancrem Winslow's ponderous plate from blue
China, the breaking of time's haggard tide
On the huge cobwebbed print of Waterloo,
With a cracked smile across the glass. I cried
To see the Emperor's sabered eagle slide
From the clutching grenadier
Staff-officer
With the gold leaf cascading down his side—
A red dragoon, his plough-horse rearing, swayed
Back on his reins to crop
The buttercup
Bursting upon the braid.

In Memory of Arthur Winslow

I

DEATH FROM CANCER

This Easter, Arthur Winslow, less than dead,
Your people set you up in Phillips' House
To settle off your wrestling with the crab—
The claws drop flesh upon your yachting blouse
Until longshoreman Charon come and stab
Through your adjusted bed
And crush the crab. On Boston Basin, shells
Hit water by the Union Boat Club wharf:
You ponder why the coxes' squeakings dwarf
The *resurrexit dominus* of all the bells.

Grandfather Winslow, look, the swanboats coast
That island in the Public Gardens, where
The bread-stuffed ducks are brooding, where with tub
And strainer the mid-Sunday Irish scare
The sun-struck shallows for the dusky chub
This Easter, and the ghost
Of risen Jesus walks the waves to run
Arthur upon a trumpeting black swan
Beyond Charles River to the Acheron
Where the wide waters and their voyager are one.

DUNBARTON

THE STONES are yellow and the grass is gray
Past Concord by the rotten lake and hill
Where crutch and trumpet meet the limousine
And half-forgotten Starks and Winslows fill
The granite plot and the dwarf pines are green
From watching for the day
When the great year of the little yeomen come
Bringing its landed Promise and the faith
That made the Pilgrim Makers take a lathe
And point their wooden steeples lest the Word be dumb.

O fearful witnesses, your day is done:
The minister from Boston waves your shades,
Like children, out of sight and out of mind.
The first selectman of Dunbarton spreads
Wreaths of New Hampshire pine cones on the lined
Casket where the cold sun
Is melting. But, at last, the end is reached;
We start our cars. The preacher's mouthings still
Deafen my poor relations on the hill:
Their sunken landmarks echo what our fathers preached.

III

FIVE YEARS LATER

THIS Easter, Arthur Winslow, five years gone
I came to mourn you, not to praise the craft
That netted you a million dollars, late
Hosing out gold in Colorado's waste,
Then lost it all in Boston real estate.
Now from the train, at dawn
Leaving Columbus in Ohio, shell
On shell of our stark culture strikes the sun
To fill my head with all our fathers won
When Cotton Mather wrestled with the fiends from hell.

You must have hankered for our family's craft:
The block-house Edward made, the Governor,
At Marshfield, and the slight coin-silver spoons
The Sheriff beat to shame the gaunt Revere,
And General Stark's coarse bas-relief in bronze
Set on your granite shaft
In rough Dunbarton; for what else could bring
You, Arthur, to the veined and alien West
But devil's notions that your gold at least
Could give back life to men who whipped or backed the King?

IV

A PRAYER FOR MY GRANDFATHER
TO OUR LADY

Mother, for these three hundred years or more
Neither our clippers nor our slavers reached
The haven of your peace in this Bay State:
Neither my father nor his father. Beached
On these dry flats of fishy real estate,
O Mother, I implore
Your scorched, blue thunderbreasts of love to pour
Buckets of blessings on my burning head
Until I rise like Lazarus from the dead:
Lavabis nos et super nivem dealbabor.

"On Copley Square, I saw you hold the door
To Trinity, the costly Church, and saw
The painted Paradise of harps and lutes
Sink like Atlantis in the Devil's jaw
And knock the Devil's teeth out by the roots;
But when I strike for shore
I find no painted idols to adore:
Hell is burned out, heaven's harp-strings are slack.
Mother, run to the chalice, and bring back
Blood on your finger-tips for Lazarus who was poor."

Winter in Dunbarton

TIME smiling on this sundial of a world
Sweltered about the snowman and the worm,
Sacker of painted idols and the peers
Of Europe; but my cat is cold, is curled
Tight as a boulder: she no longer smears
Her catnip mouse from Christmas, for the germ—
Mindless and ice, a world against our world—
Has tamped her round of brains into her ears.

This winter all the snowmen turn to stone,
Or, sick of the long hurly-burly, rise
Like butterflies into Jehovah's eyes
And shift until their crystals must atone

In water. Belle, the cat that used to rat
About my father's books, is dead. All day
The wastes of snow about my house stare in
Through idle windows at the brainless cat;
The coke-barrel in the corner whimpers. May
The snow recede and red clay furrows set
In the grim grin of their erosion, in
The caterpillar tents and roadslides, fat

With muck and winter dropsy, where the tall
Snow-monster wipes the coke-fumes from his eyes
And scatters his corruption and it lies
Gaping until the fungus-eyeballs fall

Into this eldest of the seasons. Cold
Snaps the bronze toes and fingers of the Christ
My father fetched from Florence, and the dead
Chatters to nothing in the thankless ground
His father screwed from Charlie Stark and sold
To the selectmen. Cold has cramped his head
Against his heart: my father's stone is crowned
With snowflakes and the bronze-age shards of Christ.

Mary Winslow

HER IRISH maids could never spoon out mush
Or orange-juice enough; the body cools
And smiles as a sick child
Who adds up figures, and a hush
Grips at the poised relations sipping sherry
And tracking up the carpets of her four
Room kingdom. On the rigid Charles, in snow,
Charon, the Lubber, clambers from his wherry,
And stops her hideous baby-squawks and yells,
Wit's clownish afterthought. Nothing will go
Again. Even the gelded picador
Baiting the twinned runt bulls
With walrus horns before the Spanish Belles
Is veiled with all the childish bibelots.

Mary Winslow is dead. Out on the Charles
The shells hold water and their oarblades drag,
Littered with captivated ducks, and now
The bell-rope in King's Chapel Tower unsnarls
And bells the bestial cow
From Boston Common; she is dead. But stop,
Neighbor, these pillows prop
Her that her terrified and child's cold eyes
Glass what they're not: our Copley ancestress,
Grandiloquent, square-jowled and worldly-wise,
A Cleopatra in her housewife's dress;
Nothing will go again. The bells cry: "Come,
Come home," the babbling Chapel belfry cries:
"Come, Mary Winslow, come; I bell thee home."

Salem

In salem seasick spindrift drifts or skips
To the canvas flapping on the seaward panes
Until the knitting sailor stabs at ships
Nosing like sheep of Morpheus through his brain's
Asylum. Seaman, seaman, how the draft
Lashes the oily slick about your head,
Beating up whitecaps! Seaman, Charon's raft
Dumps its damned goods into the harbor-bed,—
There sewage sickens the rebellious seas.
Remember, seaman, Salem fishermen
Once hung their nimble fleets on the Great Banks.
Where was it that New England bred the men
Who quartered the Leviathan's fat flanks
And fought the British Lion to his knees?

Concord

TEN THOUSAND Fords are idle here in search
Of a tradition. Over these dry sticks—
The Minute Man, the Irish Catholics,
The ruined bridge and Walden's fished-out perch—
The belfry of the Unitarian Church
Rings out the hanging Jesus. Crucifix,
How can your whited spindling arms transfix
Mammon's unbridled industry, the lurch
For forms to harness Heraclitus' stream!
This Church is Concord—Concord where Thoreau
Named all the birds without a gun to probe
Through darkness to the painted man and bow:
The death-dance of King Philip and his scream
Whose echo girdled this imperfect globe.

Children of Light

OUR FATHERS wrung their bread from stocks and stones
And fenced their gardens with the Redman's bones;
Embarking from the Nether Land of Holland,
Pilgrims unhouseled by Geneva's night,
They planted here the Serpent's seeds of light;
And here the pivoting searchlights probe to shock
The riotous glass houses built on rock,
And candles gutter by an empty altar,
And light is where the landless blood of Cain
Is burning, burning the unburied grain.

Rebellion

THERE was rebellion, father, when the mock
French windows slammed and you hove backward, rammed
Into your heirlooms, screens, a glass-cased clock,
The highboy quaking to its toes. You damned
My arm that cast your house upon your head
And broke the chimney flintlock on your skull.
Last night the moon was full:
I dreamed the dead
Caught at my knees and fell:
And it was well
With me, my father. Then
Behemoth and Leviathan
Devoured our mighty merchants. None could arm
Or put to sea. O father, on my farm
I added field to field
And I have sealed
An everlasting pact
With Dives to contract
The world that spreads in pain;
But the world spread
When the clubbed flintlock broke my father's brain.

At a Bible House

At a Bible House
Where smoking is forbidden
By the Prophet's law,
I saw you wiry, bed-ridden,
Gone in the kidneys; raw
Onions and a louse
Twitched on the sheet before
The palsy of your white
Stubble—a Mennonite
Or die-hard Doukabor,
God-rooted, hard. You spoke
Whistling gristle-words
Half inaudible
To us: of raw-boned birds
Migrating from the smoke
Of cities, of a gull
Perched on the redwood
Thrusting short awl-shaped leaves:
Three hundred feet of love
Where the Pacific heaves
The tap-root—wise above
Man's wisdom with the food
Squeezed from three thousand years'
Standing. It is all
A moment. The trees
Grow earthward: neither good
Nor evil, hopes nor fears,
Repulsion nor desire,
Earth, water, air or fire
Will serve to stay the fall.

The Drunken Fisherman

WALLOWING in this bloody sty,
I cast for fish that pleased my eye
(Truly Jehovah's bow suspends
No pots of gold to weight its ends);
Only the blood-mouthed rainbow trout
Rose to my bait. They flopped about
My canvas creel until the moth
Corrupted its unstable cloth.

A calendar to tell the day;
A handkerchief to wave away
The gnats; a couch unstuffed with storm
Pouching a bottle in one arm;
A whiskey bottle full of worms;
And bedroom slacks: are these fit terms
To mete the worm whose molten rage
Boils in the belly of old age?

Once fishing was a rabbit's foot—
O wind blow cold, O wind blow hot,
Let suns stay in or suns step out:
Life danced a jig on the sperm-whale's spout—
The fisher's fluent and obscene
Catches kept his conscience clean.
Children, the raging memory drools
Over the glory of past pools.

Now the hot river, ebbing, hauls
Its bloody waters into holes;
A grain of sand inside my shoe
Mimics the moon that might undo
Man and Creation too; remorse,
Stinking, has puddled up its source;
Here tantrums thrash to a whale's rage.
This is the pot-hole of old age.

Is there no way to cast my hook
Out of this dynamited brook?
The Fisher's sons must cast about
When shallow waters peter out.
I will catch Christ with a greased worm,
And when the Prince of Darkness stalks
My bloodstream to its Stygian term . . .
On water the Man-Fisher walks.

The North Sea Undertaker's Complaint

Now south and south and south the mallard heads,
His green-blue bony hood echoes the green
Flats of the Weser, and the mussel beds
Are sluggish where the webbed feet spanked the lean
Eel grass to tinder in the take-off. South
Is what I think of. It seems yesterday
I slid my hearse across the river mouth
And pitched the first iced mouse into the hay.
Thirty below it is. I hear our dumb
Club-footed orphan ring the Angelus
And clank the bell-chain for St. Gertrude's choir
To wail with the dead bell the martyrdom
Of one more blue-lipped priest; the phosphorous
Melted the hammer of his heart to fire.

Napoleon Crosses the Berezina

"There will the eagles be gathered together"

HERE Charlemagne's stunted shadow plays charades
With pawns and bishops whose play-cannister
Shivers the Snowman's bones, and the Great Bear
Shuffles away to his ancestral shades,
For here Napoleon Bonaparte parades;
Hussar and cuirassier and grenadier
Ascend the tombstone steppes to Russia. Here
The eagles gather as the West invades
The Holy Land of Russia. Lord and glory
Of dragonish, unfathomed waters, rise!
Although your Berezina cannot gnaw
These soldier-plumed pontoons to matchwood, ice
Is tuning them to tumbrils, and the snow
Blazes its carrion-miles to Purgatory.

The Soldier

IN TIME of war you could not save your skin.
Where is that Ghibelline whom Dante met
On Purgatory's doorstep, without kin
To set up chantries for his God-held debt?
So far from Campaldino, no one knows
Where he is buried by the Archiano
Whose source is Camaldoli, through the snows,
Fuggendo a piedi e sanguinando il piano,
The soldier drowned face downward in his blood.
Until the thaw he waited, then the flood
Roared like a wounded dragon over shoal
And reef and snatched away his crucifix
And rolled his body like a log to Styx;
Two angels fought with bill-hooks for his soul.

War

(AFTER RIMBAUD)

Where basilisk and mortar lob their lead
Whistling against the cloud sheep overhead,
Scarlet or green, before their black-tongued Sire,
The massed battalions flounder into fire
Until the furnace of affliction turns
A hundred thousand men to stone and burns
The poor dead in the summer grass. Their friend,
The earth, was low and thrifty to this end:
It is a god untouched by papal bulls,
The great gold chalice and the thuribles:
Cradled on its hosannahs, it will rock,
Dead to the world, until their mother, fat
With weeping underneath her cracked black hat,
Hands it her penny knotted in a sock.

Charles the Fifth and the Peasant

(AFTER VALÉRY)

ELECTED Kaiser, burgher and a knight,
Clamped in his black and burly harness, Charles
Canters on Titian's sunset to his night;
A wounded wolfhound bites his spurs and snarls:
So middle-aged and common, it's absurd
To picture him as Caesar, the first cause
Behind whose leg-of-mutton beard, the jaws
Grate on the flesh and gristle of the Word.

The fir trees in the background buzz and lurch
To the disgruntled sing-song of their fears:
"How can we stop it, stop it, stop it?" sing
The needles; and the peasant, braining perch
Against a bucket, rocks and never hears
His Ark drown in the deluge of the King.

The Shako

(AFTER RILKE)

NIGHT and its muffled creakings, as the wheels
Of Blücher's caissons circle with the clock;
He lifts his eyes and drums until he feels
The clavier shudder and allows the rock
And Scylla of her eyes to fix his face:
It is as though he looks into a glass
Reflecting on this guilty breathing-space
His terror and the salvos of the brass
From Brandenburg. She moves away. Instead,
Wearily by the broken altar, Abel
Remembers how the brothers fell apart
And hears the friendless hacking of his heart,
And strangely foreign on the mirror-table
Leans the black shako with its white death's-head.

France

My human brothers who live after me,
See how I hang. My bones eat through the skin
And flesh they carried here upon the chin
And lipping clutch of their cupidity;
Now here, now there, the starling and the sea
Gull splinter the groined eyeballs of my sin,
Brothers, more beaks of birds than needles in
The fathoms of the Bayeux Tapestry:
"God wills it, wills it, wills it: it is blood."
My brothers, if I call you brothers, see:
The blood of Abel crying from the dead
Sticks to my blackened skull and eyes. What good
Are *lebensraum* and bread to Abel dead
And rotten on the cross-beams of the tree?

1790

(FROM THE MEMOIRS OF GENERAL THIEBAULT)

ON MAUNDY THURSDAY when the King and Queen
Had washed and wiped the chosen poor and fed
Them from a boisterous wooden platter; here
We stood in forage-caps upon the green:
Green guardsmen of the Nation and its head.
The King walked out into the biting air,
Two gentlemen went with him; as they neared
Our middle gate, we stood aside for welcome;
A stone's throw lay between us when they cleared
Two horse-shoe flights of steps and crossed the Place Vendome.

"What a dog's life it is to be a king,"
I grumbled and unslung my gun; the chaff
And cinders whipped me and began to sting.
I heard our Monarch's Breughel-peasant laugh
Exploding, as a spaniel mucked with tar
Cut by his Highness' ankles on the double-quick
To fetch its stamping mistress. Louis smashed
Its backbone with a backstroke of his stick:
Slouching a little more than usual, he splashed
As boyish as a stallion to the Champs de Mars.

Between the Porch and the Altar

I

MOTHER AND SON

Meeting his mother makes him lose ten years,
Or is it twenty? Time, no doubt, has ears
That listen to the swallowed serpent, wound
Into its bowels, but he thinks no sound
Is possible before her, he thinks the past
Is settled. It is honest to hold fast
Merely to what one sees with one's own eyes
When the red velvet curves and haunches rise
To blot him from the pretty driftwood fire's
Façade of welcome. Then the son retires
Into the sack and selfhood of the boy
Who clawed through fallen houses of his Troy,
Homely and human only when the flames
Crackle in recollection. Nothing shames
Him more than this uncoiling, counterfeit
Body presented as an idol. It
Is something in a circus, big as life,
The painted dragon, a mother and a wife
With flat glass eyes pushed at him on a stick;
The human mover crawls to make them click.
The forehead of her father's portrait peels
With rosy dryness, and the schoolboy kneels
To ask the benediction of the hand,
Lifted as though to motion him to stand,
Dangling its watch-chain on the Holy Book—
A little golden snake that mouths a hook.

II

ADAM AND EVE

THE FARMER sizzles on his shaft all day.
He is content and centuries away
From white-hot Concord, and he stands on guard.
Or is he melting down like sculptured lard?
His hand is crisp and steady on the plough.
I quarrelled with you, but am happy now
To while away my life for your unrest
Of terror. Never to have lived is best;
Man tasted Eve with death. I taste my wife
And children while I hold your hands. I knife
Their names into this elm. What is exempt?
I eye the statue with an awed contempt
And see the puritanical façade
Of the white church that Irish exiles made
For Patrick—that Colonial from Rome
Had magicked the charmed serpents from their home,
As though he were the Piper. Will his breath
Scorch the red dragon of my nerves to death?
By sundown we are on a shore. You walk
A little way before me and I talk,
Half to myself and half aloud. They lied,
My cold-eyed seedy fathers when they died,
Or rather threw their lives away, to fix
Sterile, forbidding nameplates on the bricks
Above a kettle. Jesus rest their souls!
You cry for help. Your market-basket rolls
With all its baking apples in the lake.
You watch the whorish slither of a snake
That chokes a duckling. When we try to kiss,
Our eyes are slits and cringing, and we hiss;
Scales glitter on our bodies as we fall.
The Farmer melts upon his pedestal.

III

KATHERINE'S DREAM

It MUST have been a Friday. I could hear
The top-floor typist's thunder and the beer
That you had brought in cases hurt my head;
I'd sent the pillows flying from my bed,
I hugged my knees together and I gasped.
The dangling telephone receiver rasped
Like someone in a dream who cannot stop
For breath or logic till his victim drop
To darkness and the sheets. I must have slept,
But still could hear my father who had kept
Your guilty presents but cut off my hair.
He whispers that he really doesn't care
If I am your kept woman all my life,
Or ruin your two children and your wife;
But my dishonor makes him drink. Of course
I'll tell the court the truth for his divorce.
I walk through snow into St. Patrick's yard.
Black nuns with glasses smile and stand on guard
Before a bulkhead in a bank of snow,
Whose charred doors open, as good people go
Inside by twos to the confessor. One
Must have a friend to enter there, but none
Is friendless in this crowd, and the nuns smile.
I stand aside and marvel; for a while
The winter sun is pleasant and it warms
My heart with love for others, but the swarms
Of penitents have dwindled. I begin
To cry and ask God's pardon of our sin.

Where are you? You were with me and are gone.
All the forgiven couples hurry on
To dinner and their nights, and none will stop.
I run about in circles till I drop
Against a padlocked bulkhead in a yard
Where faces redden and the snow is hard.

IV

AT THE ALTAR

I sit at a gold table with my girl
Whose eyelids burn with brandy. What a whirl
Of Easter eggs is colored by the lights,
As the Norwegian dancer's crystalled tights
Flash with her naked leg's high-booted skate,
Like Northern Lights upon my watching plate.
The twinkling steel above me is a star;
I am a fallen Christmas tree. Our car
Races through seven red-lights—then the road
Is unpatrolled and empty, and a load
Of ply-wood with a tail-light makes us slow.
I turn and whisper in her ear. You know
I want to leave my mother and my wife,
You wouldn't have me tied to them for life . . .
Time runs, the windshield runs with stars. The past
Is cities from a train, until at last
Its escalating and black-windowed blocks
Recoil against a Gothic church. The clocks
Are tolling. I am dying. The shocked stones
Are falling like a ton of bricks and bones
That snap and splinter and descend in glass
Before a priest who mumbles through his Mass
And sprinkles holy water; and the Day
Breaks with its lightning on the man of clay,
Dies amara valde. Here the Lord
Is Lucifer in harness: hand on sword,
He watches me for Mother, and will turn
The bier and baby-carriage where I burn.

To Peter Taylor on the Feast of the Epiphany

Peter, the war has taught me to revere
The rulers of this darkness, for I fear
That only Armageddon will suffice
To turn the hero skating on thin ice
When Whore and Beast and Dragon rise for air
From allegoric waters. Fear is where
We hunger: where the Irishmen recall
How wisdom trailed a star into a stall
And knelt in sacred terror to confer
Its fabulous gold and frankincense and myrrh:
And where the lantern-noses scrimmage down
The highway to the sea below this town
And the sharp barker rigs his pre-war planes
To lift old Adam's dollars for his pains;
There on the thawing ice, in red and white
And blue, the bugs are buzzing for the flight.
December's daylight hours have gone their round
Of sorrows with the sun into the sound,
And still the grandsires battle through the slush
To storm the landing biplanes with a rush—
Until their cash and somersaulting snare
Fear with its fingered stop-watch in mid-air.

As a Plane Tree by the Water

DARKNESS has called to darkness, and disgrace
Elbows about our windows in this planned
Babel of Boston where our money talks
And multiplies the darkness of a land
Of preparation where the Virgin walks
And roses spiral her enamelled face
Or fall to splinters on unwatered streets.
Our Lady of Babylon, go by, go by,
I was once the apple of your eye;
Flies, flies are on the plane tree, on the streets.

The flies, the flies, the flies of Babylon
Buzz in my ear-drums while the devil's long
Dirge of the people detonates the hour
For floating cities where his golden tongue
Enchants the masons of the Babel Tower
To raise tomorrow's city to the sun
That never sets upon these hell-fire streets
Of Boston, where the sunlight is a sword
Striking at the withholder of the Lord:
Flies, flies are on the plane tree, on the streets.

Flies strike the miraculous waters of the iced
Atlantic and the eyes of Bernadette
Who saw Our Lady standing in the cave
At Massabielle, saw her so squarely that
Her vision put out reason's eyes. The grave
Is open-mouthed and swallowed up in Christ.
O walls of Jericho! And all the streets
To our Atlantic wall are singing: "Sing,
Sing for the resurrection of the King."
Flies, flies are on the plane tree, on the streets.

The Crucifix

How DRY time screaks in its fat axle-grease,
As spare November strikes us through the ice
And the Leviathan breaks water in the rice
Fields, at the poles, at the hot gates to Greece;
It's time: the old unmastered lion roars
And ramps like a mad dog outside the doors,
Snapping at gobbets in my thumbless hand.
The seaways lurch through Sodom's knees of sand
Tomorrow. We are sinking. "Run, rat, run,"
The prophets thunder, and I run upon
My father, Adam. Adam, if our land
Become the desolation of a hand
That shakes the Temple back to clay, how can
War ever change my old into new man?
Get out from under my feet, old man. Let me pass;
On Ninth Street, through the Hallowe'en's soaped glass,
I picked at an old bone on two crossed sticks
And found, to *Via et Vita et Veritas*
A stray dog's signpost is a crucifix.

Dea Roma

Aᴜɢᴜsᴛᴜs mended you. He hung the tongue
Of Tullius upon your rostrum, lashed
The money-lenders from your Senate-house;
And Brutus bled his forty-six per cent
For *Pax Romana*. Quiet as a mouse
Blood licks the king's cosmetics with its tongue.

Some years, your legions soldiered through this world
Under the eagles of Lord Lucifer;
But human torches lit the captains home
Where victims warped the royal crucifix:
How many roads and sewers led to Rome.
Satan is pacing up and down the world

These sixteen centuries, Eternal City,
That we have squandered since Maxentius fell
Under the Milvian Bridge; from the dry dome
Of Michelangelo, your fisherman
Walks on the waters of a draining Rome
To bank his catch in the Celestial City.

The Ghost

(AFTER SEXTUS PROPERTIUS)

A GHOST is someone: death has left a hole
For the lead-colored soul to beat the fire:
    Cynthia leaves her dirty pyre
    And seems to coil herself and roll
        Under my canopy,
Love's stale and public playground, where I lie
And fill the run-down empire of my bed.
I see the street, her potter's field, is red
And lively with the ashes of the dead;

But she no longer sparkles off in smoke:
It is the body carted to the gate
    Last Friday, when the sizzling grate
    Left its charred furrows on her smock
        And ate into her hip.
A black nail dangles from a finger-tip
And Lethe oozes from her nether lip.
Her thumb-bones rattle on her brittle hands,
As Cynthia stamps and hisses and demands:

"Sextus, has sleep already washed away
Your manhood? You forget the window-sill
    My sliding wore to slivers? Day
    Would break before the Seven Hills
        Saw Cynthia retreat
And climb your shoulders to the knotted sheet.
You shouldered me and galloped on bare feet
To lay me by the crossroads. Have no fear:
Notus, who snatched your promise, has no ear.

"But why did no one call in my deaf ear?
Your calling would have gained me one more day.
　　Sextus, although you ran away
　　You might have called and stopped my bier
　　　　A second by your door.
No tears drenched a black toga for your whore
When broken tilestones bruised her face before
The Capitol. Would it have strained your purse
To scatter ten cheap roses on my hearse?

"The State will make Pompilia's Chloris burn:
I knew her secret when I kissed the skull
　　Of Pluto in the tainted bowl.
　　Let Nomas burn her books and turn
　　　　Her poisons into gold;
The finger-prints upon the potsherd told
Her love. You let a slut, whose body sold
To Thracians, liquefy my golden bust
In the coarse flame that crinkled me to dust.

"If Chloris' bed has left you with your head,
Lover, I think you'll answer my arrears:
　　My nurse is getting on in years,
　　See that she gets a little bread—
　　　　She never clutched your purse;
See that my little humpback hears no curse
From her close-fisted friend. But burn the verse
You bellowed half a lifetime in my name:
Why should you feed me to the fires of fame?

"I will not hound you, much as you have earned
It, Sextus: I shall reign in your four books—
    I swear this by the Hag who looks
    Into my heart where it was burned:
        Propertius, I kept faith;
If not, may serpents suck my ghost to death
And spit it with their forked and killing breath
Into the Styx where Agamemnon's wife
Founders in the green circles of her life.

"Beat the sycophant ivy from my urn,
That twists its binding shoots about my bones
    Where apple-sweetened Anio drones
    Through orchards that will never burn
        While honest Herakles,
My patron, watches. Anio, you will please
Me if you whisper upon sliding knees:
'Propertius, Cynthia is here:
She shakes her blossoms when my waters clear.'

"You cannot turn your back upon a dream,
For phantoms have their reasons when they come:
    We wander midnights: then the numb
    Ghost wades from the Lethean stream;
        Even the foolish dog
Stops its hell-raising mouths and casts its clog;
At cock-crow Charon checks us in his log.
Others can have you, Sextus; I alone
Hold: and I grind your manhood bone on bone."

In the Cage

THE LIFERS file into the hall,
According to their houses—twos
Of laundered denim. On the wall
A colored fairy tinkles blues
And titters by the balustrade;
Canaries beat their bars and scream.
We come from tunnels where the spade
Pick-axe and hod for plaster steam
In mud and insulation. Here
The Bible-twisting Israelite
Fasts for his Harlem. It is night,
And it is vanity, and age
Blackens the heart of Adam. Fear,
The yellow chirper, beaks its cage.

At the Indian Killer's Grave

"Here, also, are the veterans of King Philip's War,
who burned villages and slaughtered young and old,
with pious fierceness, while the godly souls through-
out the land were helping them with prayer."

HAWTHORNE.

Behind King's Chapel what the earth has kept
Whole from the jerking noose of time extends
Its dark enigma to Jehoshaphat;
Or will King Philip plait
The just man's scalp in the wailing valley! Friends,
Blacker than these black stones the subway bends
About the dirty elm roots and the well
For the unchristened infants in the waste
Of the great garden rotten to its root;
Death, the engraver, puts forward his bone foot
And Grace-with-wings and Time-on-wings compel
All this antique abandon of the disgraced
To face Jehovah's buffets and his ends.

The dusty leaves and frizzled lilacs gear
This garden of the elders with baroque
And prodigal embellishments but smoke,
Settling upon the pilgrims and their grounds,
Espouses and confounds
Their dust with the off-scourings of the town;
The libertarian crown
Of England built their mausoleum. Here
A clutter of Bible and weeping willows guards
The stern Colonial magistrates and wards
Of Charles the Second, and the clouds
Weep on the just and unjust as they will,—
For the poor dead cannot see Easter crowds
On Boston Common or the Beacon Hill
Where strangers hold the golden Statehouse dome
For good and always. Where they live is home:
A common with an iron railing: here
Frayed cables wreathe the spreading cenotaph
Of John and Mary Winslow and the laugh
Of Death is hacked in sandstone, in their year.

A green train grinds along its buried tracks
And screeches. When the great mutation racks
The Pilgrim Fathers' relics, will these placques
Harness the spare-ribbed persons of the dead
To battle with the dragon? Philip's head
Grins on the platter, fouls in pantomime
The fingers of kept time:
"Surely, this people is but grass,"
He whispers, "this will pass;
But, Sirs, the trollop dances on your skulls
And breaks the hollow noddle like an egg
That thought the world an eggshell. Sirs, the gulls
Scream from the squelching wharf-piles, beg a leg
To crack their crops. The Judgment is at hand;
Only the dead are poorer in this world
Where State and elders thundered *raca,* hurled
Anathemas at nature and the land
That fed the hunter's gashed and green perfection—
Its settled mass concedes no outlets for your puns
And verbal Paradises. Your election,
Hawking above this slime
For souls as single as their skeletons,
Flutters and claws in the dead hand of time."

When you go down this man-hole to the drains,
The doorman barricades you in and out;
You wait upon his pleasure. All about
The pale, sand-colored, treeless chains
Of T-squared buildings strain
To curb the spreading of the braced terrain;
When you go down this hole, perhaps your pains
Will be rewarded well; no rough-cast house
Will bed and board you in King's Chapel. Here
A public servant putters with a knife
And paints the railing red
Forever, as a mouse
Cracks walnuts by the headstones of the dead
Whose chiselled angels peer
At you, as if their art were long as life.

I ponder on the railing at this park:
Who was the man who sowed the dragon's teeth,
That fabulous or fancied patriarch
Who sowed so ill for his descent, beneath
King's Chapel in this underworld and dark?
John, Matthew, Luke and Mark,
Gospel me to the Garden, let me come
Where Mary twists the warlock with her flowers—
Her soul a bridal chamber fresh with flowers
And her whole body an ecstatic womb,
As through the trellis peers the sudden Bridegroom.

Mr. Edwards and the Spider

I saw the spiders marching through the air,
Swimming from tree to tree that mildewed day
   In latter August when the hay
   Came creaking to the barn. But where
     The wind is westerly,
Where gnarled November makes the spiders fly
Into the apparitions of the sky,
They purpose nothing but their ease and die
Urgently beating east to sunrise and the sea;

What are we in the hands of the great God?
It was in vain you set up thorn and briar
   In battle array against the fire
   And treason crackling in your blood;
     For the wild thorns grow tame
And will do nothing to oppose the flame;
Your lacerations tell the losing game
You play against a sickness past your cure.
How will the hands be strong? How will the heart endure?

A very little thing, a little worm,
Or hourglass-blazoned spider, it is said,
   Can kill a tiger. Will the dead
   Hold up his mirror and affirm
     To the four winds the smell
And flash of his authority? It's well
If God who holds you to the pit of hell,
Much as one holds a spider, will destroy,
Baffle and dissipate your soul. As a small boy

On Windsor Marsh, I saw the spider die
When thrown into the bowels of fierce fire:
    There's no long struggle, no desire
    To get up on its feet and fly—
        It stretches out its feet
And dies. This is the sinner's last retreat;
Yes, and no strength exerted on the heat
Then sinews the abolished will, when sick
And full of burning, it will whistle on a brick.

    But who can plumb the sinking of that soul?
    Josiah Hawley, picture yourself cast
        Into a brick-kiln where the blast
        Fans your quick vitals to a coal—
            If measured by a glass,
    How long would it seem burning! Let there pass
    A minute, ten, ten trillion; but the blaze
    Is infinite, eternal: this is death,
To die and know it. This is the Black Widow, death.

After the Surprising Conversions

September twenty-second, Sir: today
I answer. In the latter part of May,
Hard on our Lord's Ascension, it began
To be more sensible. A gentleman
Of more than common understanding, strict
In morals, pious in behavior, kicked
Against our goad. A man of some renown,
An useful, honored person in the town,
He came of melancholy parents; prone
To secret spells, for years they kept alone—
His uncle, I believe, was killed of it:
Good people, but of too much or little wit.
I preached one Sabbath on a text from Kings;
He showed concernment for his soul. Some things
In his experience were hopeful. He
Would sit and watch the wind knocking a tree
And praise this countryside our Lord has made.
Once when a poor man's heifer died, he laid
A shilling on the doorsill; though a thirst
For loving shook him like a snake, he durst
Not entertain much hope of his estate
In heaven. Once we saw him sitting late
Behind his attic window by a light
That guttered on his Bible; through that night
He meditated terror, and he seemed
Beyond advice or reason, for he dreamed
That he was called to trumpet Judgment Day
To Concord. In the latter part of May
He cut his throat. And though the coroner
Judged him delirious, soon a noisome stir

Palsied our village. At Jehovah's nod
Satan seemed more let loose amongst us: God
Abandoned us to Satan, and he pressed
Us hard, until we thought we could not rest
Till we had done with life. Content was gone.
All the good work was quashed. We were undone.
The breath of God had carried out a planned
And sensible withdrawal from this land;
The multitude, once unconcerned with doubt,
Once neither callous, curious nor devout,
Jumped at broad noon, as though some peddler groaned
At it in its familiar twang: "My friend,
Cut your own throat. Cut your own throat. Now! Now!"
September twenty-second, Sir, the bough
Cracks with the unpicked apples, and at dawn
The small-mouth bass breaks water, gorged with spawn.

The Slough of Despond

AT SUNSET only swamp
Afforded pursey tufts of grass . . . these gave,
I sank. Each humus-sallowed pool
Rattled its cynic's lamp
And croaked: "We lay Apollo in his grave;
Narcissus is our fool."

My God, it was a slow
And brutal push! At last I struck the tree
Whose dead and purple arms, entwined
With sterile thorns, said: "Go!
Pluck me up by the roots and shoulder me;
The watchman's eyes are blind."

My arms swung like an axe.
And with my tingling sword I lopped the knot:
The labyrinthine East was mine
But for the asking. Lax
And limp, the creepers caught me by the foot,
And then I toed their line;

I walk upon the flood:
My way is wayward; there is no way out:
Now how the weary waters swell,—
The tree is down in blood!
All the bats of Babel flap about
The rising sun of hell.

The Blind Leading the Blind

NOTHING will hustle: at his own sweet time
My father and his before him humanized
· The seedy fields and heaped them on my house
Of straw; no flaring, hurtling thing surprised
Us out of season, and the corn-fed mouse
Reined in his bestial passions. Hildesheim
Survived the passing angel; who'd require
Our passion for the Easter? Satan snored
By the brass railing, while his back-log roared
And coiled its vapors on St. Gertrude's blue stone spire:

A land of mattocks; here the brothers strode,
Hulking as horses in their worsted hose
And cloaks and shin-guards—each had hooked his hoe
Upon his fellow's shoulder; by each nose
The aimless waterlines of eyeballs show
Their greenness. They are blind—blind to the road
And to its Maker. Here my father saw
The leadman trip against a pigpen, crash,
Legs spread, his codpiece split, his fiddle smash . . .
These mammoth vintners danced their blood out in the straw.

The Fens

(AFTER COBBETT)

FROM Crowland to St. Edmund's to Ipswich
The fens are level as a drawing-board:
Great bowling greens divided by a ditch—
The grass as thick as grows on ground. The Lord
High Sheriff settles here, as on a sea,
When the parochial calm of sunset chills
The world to its four corners. And the hills
Are green with hops and harvest, and a bitch
Spuddles about a vineyard on a tree;

Here everything grows well. Here the fat land
Has no stone bigger than a ladybug,
No milkweed or wild onion can withstand
The sheriff's men, and sunlight sweats the slug.
Here the rack-renting system has its say:
At nightfall sheep as fat as hogs shall lie
Heaped on the mast and corncobs of the sty
And they will rise and take the landlord's hand;
The bailiff bears the Bell, the Bell, away.

The Death of the Sheriff

"forsitan et Priami fuerint quae fata, requiras?"

I

NOLI ME TANGERE

We park and stare. A full sky of the stars
Wheels from the pumpkin setting of the moon
And sparks the windows of the yellow farm
Where the red-flannelled madmen look through bars
At windmills thrashing snowflakes by an arm
Of the Atlantic. Soon
The undertaker who collects antiques
Will let his motor idle at the door
And set his pine-box on the parlor floor.
Our homicidal sheriff howled for weeks;

We kiss. The State had reasons: on the whole,
It acted out of kindness when it locked
Its servant in this place and had him watched
Until an ordered darkness left his soul
A *tabula rasa;* when the Angel knocked
The sheriff laid his notched
Revolver on the table for the guest.
Night draws us closer in its bearskin wrap
And our loved sightless smother feels the tap
Of the blind stars descending to the west

71

To lay the Devil in the pit our hands
Are draining like a windmill. Who'll atone
For the unsearchable quicksilver heart
Where spiders stare their eyes out at their own
Spitting and knotted likeness? We must start:
Our aunt, his mother, stands
Singing *O Rock of Ages,* as the light
Wanderers show a man with a white cane
Who comes to take the coffin in his wain,
The thirsty Dipper on the arc of night.

II

THE PORTRAIT

THE WHISKEY circulates, until I smash
The candelabrum from the mantel's top,
And scorch Poseidon on the panel where
He forks the blocks of Troy into the air.
A chipmunk shucks the strychnine in a cup;
The popping pine-cones flash
Like shore-bait on his face in oils. My bile
Rises, and beads of perspiration swell
To flies and splash the *Parmachenie Belle*
That I am scraping with my uncle's file.

I try the barb upon a pencilled line
Of Vergil. Nothing underneath the sun
Has bettered, Uncle, since the scaffolds flamed
On butchered Troy until Aeneas shamed
White Helen on her hams by Vesta's shrine . . .
All that the Greeks have won
I'll cancel with a sidestroke of my sword;
Now I can let my father, wife and son
Banquet Apollo for Laomedon:
Helen will satiate the fire, my Lord.

I search the starlight . . . Helen will appear,
Pura per noctem in luce . . . I am chilled,
I drop the barbless fly into my purse
Beside his nickel shield. It is God's curse,
God's, that has purpled Lucifer with fear
And burning. God has willed;
I lift the window. Digging has begun,
The hill road sparkles, and the mourners' cars
Wheel with the whited sepulchres of stars
To light the worldly dead-march of the sun.

The Dead in Europe

After the planes unloaded, we fell down
Buried together, unmarried men and women;
Not crown of thorns, not iron, not Lombard crown,
Not grilled and spindle spires pointing to heaven
Could save us. Raise us, Mother, we fell down
Here hugger-mugger in the jellied fire:
Our sacred earth in our day was our curse.

Our Mother, shall we rise on Mary's day
In Maryland, wherever corpses married
Under the rubble, bundled together? Pray
For us whom the blockbusters marred and buried;
When Satan scatters us on Rising-day,
O Mother, snatch our bodies from the fire:
Our sacred earth in our day was our curse.

Mother, my bones are trembling and I hear
The earth's reverberations and the trumpet
Bleating into my shambles. Shall I bear,
(O Mary!) unmarried man and powder-puppet,
Witness to the Devil? Mary, hear,
O Mary, marry earth, sea, air and fire;
Our sacred earth in our day is our curse.

Where the Rainbow Ends

I saw the sky descending, black and white,
Not blue, on Boston where the winters wore
The skulls to jack-o'-lanterns on the slates,
And Hunger's skin-and-bone retrievers tore
The chickadee and shrike. The thorn tree waits
Its victim and tonight
The worms will eat the deadwood to the foot
Of Ararat: the scythers, Time and Death,
Helmed locusts, move upon the tree of breath;
The wild ingrafted olive and the root

Are withered, and a winter drifts to where
The Pepperpot, ironic rainbow, spans
Charles River and its scales of scorched-earth miles.
I saw my city in the Scales, the pans
Of judgment rising and descending. Piles
Of dead leaves char the air—
And I am a red arrow on this graph
Of Revelations. Every dove is sold
The Chapel's sharp-shinned eagle shifts its hold
On serpent-Time, the rainbow's epitaph.

In Boston serpents whistle at the cold.
The victim climbs the altar steps and sings:
"Hosannah to the lion, lamb, and beast
Who fans the furnace-face of IS with wings:
I breathe the ether of my marriage feast."
At the high altar, gold
And a fair cloth. I kneel and the wings beat
My cheek. What can the dove of Jesus give
You now but wisdom, exile? Stand and live,
The dove has brought an olive branch to eat.

The Mills of the Kavanaughs

For my mother,
and in memory of my father

These poems have appeared in *The Kenyon Review, The Nation, Poetry* and *Partisan Review* and, excepting the title poem, in *Poems: 1938–1949,* published by Messrs. Faber and Faber, London. "The Fat Man in the Mirror" is not a translation but an imitation.

The Mills of the Kavanaughs

"Ah, love let us be true
To one another! for the world, which seems
To lie before us like a land of dreams . . ."
[DOVER BEACH]
"Morals are the memory of success that no longer succeeds."
[IN THE AMERICAN GRAIN]

An afternoon in the fall of 1943; a village a little north of Bath, Maine. Anne Kavanaugh is sitting in her garden playing solitaire. She pretends that the Bible she has placed in the chair opposite her is her opponent. At one end of the garden is the grave of her husband, Harry Kavanaugh, a naval officer who was retired after Pearl Harbor. The Kavanaughs are a Catholic family that came to Maine in the 17th century. Their house is called *Kavanaugh;* it is on a hill, and at its foot, there is a mill pond, and by it a marble statue of Persephone, the goddess who become a queen by becoming queen of the dead. The Abnakis, or Penobscots, are almost extinct Maine Indians, who were originally converted by the French. Anne comes of a poor family. She was adopted by the Kavanaughs many years before she married. Most of the poem is a revery of her childhood and marriage, and is addressed to her dead husband.

THE Douay Bible on the garden chair
Facing the lady playing solitaire
In blue-jeans and a sealskin toque from Bath
Is *Sol,* her dummy. There's a sort of path
Or rut of weeds that serpents down a hill
And graveyard to a ruined burlap mill;
There, a maternal nineteenth century
Italian statue of Persephone
Still beckons to a mob of Bacchanals
To plunge like dogs or athletes through the falls,
And fetch her the stone garland she will hurl.
The lady drops her cards. She kneels to furl
Her husband's flag, and thinks his mound and stone
Are like a buried bed. "This is the throne
They must have willed us. Harry, not a thing
Was missing: we were children of a king.

"Our people had kept up their herring weirs,
Their rum and logging grants two hundred years,
When Cousin Franklin Pierce was President—
Almost three hundred, Harry, when you sent
His signed engraving sailing on your kite
Above the gable, where your mother's light,
A daylight bulb in tortoise talons, pipped
The bull-mad june-bugs on the manuscript
That she was typing to redeem our mills
From Harding's taxes, and we lost our means
Of drawing pulp and water from those hills
Above the Saco, where our tenants drilled
Abnaki partisans for Charles the First,
And seated our Republicans, while Hearst
And yellow paper fed the moose that swilled
Our spawning ponds for weeds like spinach greens.

"Love, is it trespassing to call them ours?
They are now. Once I trespassed—picking flowers
For keepsakes of my journey, once I bent
Above your well, where lawn and battlement
Were trembling, yet without a flaw to mar
Their sweet surrender. Ripples seemed to star
My face, the rocks, the bottom of the well;
My heart, pursued by all its plunder, fell,
And I was tossing petals from my lair
Of copper leaves above your mother's chair.
Alone in that *verboten,* how I mocked
Her erudition, while she read and rocked.
And how I queened it, when she let me lop
At pigeons with my lilliputian crop,
And pester squirrels from that beech tree's bole
Colored with bunting like a barber's pole."

The lady sees the statues in the pool.
She dreams and thinks, "My husband was a fool
To run out from the Navy when disgrace
Still wanted zeal to look him in the face."
She wonders why her fancy makes her look
Across the table, where the open Book
Forgets the ease and honor of its shelf
To tell her that her gambling with herself
Is love of self. She pauses, drops the deck,
And feels her husband's fingers touch her neck.
She thinks of Daphne—Daphne could outrun
The birds, and saw her swiftness tire the sun,
And yet, perhaps, saw nothing to admire
Beneath Apollo, when his crackling fire
Stood rooted, half unwilling to undo
Her laurel branches dropping from the blue.

The leaves, sun's yellow, listen, Love, they fall.
She hears her husband, and she tries to call
Him, then remembers. Burning stubble roars
About the garden. Columns fill the life
Insurance calendar on which she scores.
The lady laughs. She shakes her parasol.
The table rattles, and she chews her pearled,
Once telescopic pencil, till its knife
Snaps open. *"Sol,"* she whispers, laughing, *"Sol,*
If you will help me, I will win the world."
Her husband's thumbnail scratches on her comb.
A boy is pointing at the sun. He cries:
O dandelion, wish my wish, be true,
And blows the callow pollen in her eyes.
"Harry," she whispers, "we are far from home—
A boy and girl a-Maying in the blue

"Of March or April. We are tumbling through
The chalk-pits to our rural demigod,
Old skull-and-horns, the bullock Father slew,
There on the sky-line. Let the offal sod
Our fields with Ceres. Here is piety;
Ceres is here replenished to the full—
Green the clairvoyance of her deity,
Although the landscape's like a bullock's skull . . .
Things held together once," she thinks. "But where?
Not for the life of me! How can I see
Things as they are, my Love, while April steals
Through bog and chalk-pit, till these boulders bear
Persephone—illusory, perhaps,
Yet her renewal, no illusion, for this air
Is orgied, Harry, and your setter yaps
About the goddess, while it nips her heels."

The setter worries through the coils of brush
And steaming bramble, and the children rush
Hurrahing, where no marsh or scrubby field
Or sorry clump of virgin pine will yield
A moment's covert to the half-extinct
And pileated bird they trail with linked
Fingers and little burlap sacks of salt.
The bird, a wise old uncle, knows what fault
Or whimsy guides the children when they halt
For sling-stones. Too distinguished to exalt,
It drops and cruises, while the children vault
The trifling mill-stream, where it used to kill
The sandsnakes in the flotsam with its bill;
Its stoned red-tufted shadow skims the pond;
Now it is lifting, now it clears the mill,
And, tired with child's-play, sails beyond beyond.

The children splash and paddle. Then, hand in hand,
They duck for turtles. Where she cannot stand,
The whirlpool sucks her. She has set her teeth
Into his thumb. She wrestles underneath
The sea-green smother; stunned, unstrung and torn
Into a thousand globules by that horn
Or whorl of river, she has burst apart
Like churning water on her husband's heart—
A horny thumbnail! Then they lie beside
The marble goddess. "Look, the stony-eyed
Persephone has mouldered like a leaf!"
The children whisper. Old and pedestalled,
Where rock-pools used to echo when she called
Demeter—sheathed in Lincoln green, a sheaf—
The statue of Persephone regards
The river, while it moils a hundred yards

Below her garland. Here, they used to build
A fire to broil their trout. A beer can filled
With fishskins marks the dingle where they died.
They whisper, "Touch her. If her foot should slide
A little earthward, Styx will hold her down
Nella miseria, smashed to plaster, balled
Into the whirlpool's boil." Here bubbles filled
Their basin, and the children splashed. They died
In Adam, while the grass snake slid appalled
To summer, while Jehovah's grass-green lyre
Was rustling all about them in the leaves
That gurgled by them turning upside down;
The time of marriage!—worming on all fours
Up slag and deadfall, while the torrent pours
Down, down, down, down—and she, a crested bird,
Or rainbow, hovers, lest the thunder-word

Deluge her playmate in Jehovah's beard
Of waterfalls. She listens to his feared
Footsteps, no longer muffled by the green
Torrent, that serpents up and down between
Them, while she sprints along the shelf.
Her toes curl. "I am married to myself,"
She hears him shout, and answers, "All for us."
And *ah, ah, ah* echoes the cavernous
Cascading froth's crescendo: *Stammerer,*
You cannot answer, Child, you cannot answer.
She wades. The boy, too small to follow her,
Calls out in anger, and three times her answer
Struggles to tell him, but her bubbles star
The cheerful surface idly. She is part
Of the down-under beating like her heart.
Although the voice is near her, it sounds far.

"The world hushed. Dying in your arms, I heard
The mowers moving through that golden-eared
Avernal ambush, and I seemed to hear
The harvesters, who rose to volunteer
As escorts for Persephone's deferred
Renewal of the earth, so vainly feared;
And all their voices, light as feathers, sighed
Unwelcome to that violated bride,
Uncertain even of her hold on hell,
Who curbed her horses, as if serpent-stung,
While shadows massed in earnest to rebel.
Weary and glorious, once, when time was young,
She ran from Hades. All Avernus burned.
Black horse and chariot thundered at her heel.
She, fleeting earthward, nothing seemed to steal,
But the fruition that her hell had earned.

"On days of Obligation, if our farm
Stockaded by wild cherries, and the spruce
My father hacked like weeds to keep us warm
Through summer, if it crossed your path; what use
Was it? His thirteen children and his goat,
Those cook-stove heated clapboards, where we slept
In relays, beaver dams of cans, a moat
Our cesspool drained on—if on that, he kept
A second woman twenty farms up road;
What use was it? The air we breathed he owed
The poor-box. Is it throwing money down
A well to help the poor? They die. They glitter
Like a cathedral—whiskey, tears and tapers.
He died. Your mother came and signed my papers.
She plucked me like a kitten from that litter,
And charged my board and lodging to the town.

"Your house, can you forget it? Or its *school,*
Where Bowdoin students taught us cowboy pool—
Brother and sister! How Abnakis, screened
In bleeding sumac, scared us, when they leaned
Against us—pocked and warlocked—to pursue
Their weaponed shadows raiding through the dew
Of twilight after crickets? How we spiked
Our bows with pears for flinging? When we hiked
Homeward, you winged our falcon with a rock—
Fumbling for the tail-feathers of a cock,
Blue-blooded, gluttonous, it swallowed blood,
While mother fetched its parrot perch and hood,
And set it by the daub of Kavanaugh,
Sheriff for Lincoln County and the King,
Whose old two-handed eighteenth century saw
Hung like a whale's jaw lashed with bits of string.

"The blazings of the woodsman left a track
Straight as an arrow to the blacksmith's shack
Where I was born. There, just a month before
Our marriage, I can see you: we had dressed
Ourselves in holly, and you cut your crest,
A stump and green shoots on my father's door,
And swore our marriage would renew the cleft
Forests and skulls of the Abnakis left
Like saurian footprints by the lumber lord,
Who broke their virgin greenness cord by cord
To build his clearing. Once his axe was law
And culture, but this house in its decline
Forgets how tender green shoots used to spring
From the decaying stump—Red Kavanaugh
Who built it, and inscribed its Latin line:
Cut down we flourish, on his signet ring.

"And there was greenwood spitting on the fire-dogs,
That looked like Hessians. It was June, and Maine
Smouldered to greenness, and the perching frogs
Chirred to the greener sizzle of a rain
That freshened juniper and Wilson's thrush
Before the Revolution. We were hot,
And climbed the Portland wagon-road to push
Past vineyards to the *praying niggers'* lot.
There, the Abnakis, christened by the French,
Chanted our *Miserere.* Love, how wild,
Their fragrance! Grouse were pecking on their trench—
Red Kavanaugh's, who burned and buried child
And squaw and elder in their river bed,
A pine-tree shilling a scalp; yes, scalped their king
In the dead drop—and both already dead,
Drowned in the dazzling staidness of our spring.

"Marriage by drowning! Soon enough our own,"
She whispers, laughing. "Though they left no stone
Unturned to stop us, soon the maids in red
Were singing Cinderella at our mass;
They called me Cinderella, but I said:
'Prince Charming is my shadow in the glass.' "
The lady stacks her cards. She laughs and scores.
She dreams. Her husband holds his mansion doors
Open. He helps the bridesmaids, stoops to tie
Her roses. "Anne," he teases, "Anne, my whole
House is your serf. The squirrel in its hole
Who hears your patter, Anne, and sinks its eye-
Teeth, bigger than a human's, in its treasure
Of rotten shells, is wiser far than I
Who have forsaken all my learning's leisure
To be your man and husband—God knows why!"

"God knows," she wonders, "when I watched you sail
From Boston Harbor on the *Arkansas*
For the Pacific, I was glad. No mail
Until December. You returned. I saw
Your horses pulling up the hill, and heard
You crying like a white, bewildered bird
The sea rejected. You were on the floor,
And clowning like a boy. You grimaced, bared
Your chest, and bellowed, 'Listen, undeclared
War seems to . . . static . . . the United States
And Honolulu are at war. War, War!
Pearl Harbor's burning!' But I knew you cared
Little, and that was why you turned to creak
The rusty hinges of the oven door.
You creaked and puttered, till I thought our plates
Of numbered birds would smash their frames, and shriek.

"The horses stumbled, and we had to stop.
The mountain soared. Its top, the Widow's Walk,
A mile above us, balanced on a drop,
Where dryfall after dryfall crashed to chalk.
The roots were charcoal. Standing shells of stocks
At each meander marched to block our climb
Along a snake-trail weighted down with rocks.
This was Avernus. There, about this time,
Demeter's daughter first reviewed the dead—
Most doomed and pompous, while the maples shed
Their martyr's rubric, and a torrent stood
Stock-still, reflecting; and she heard the bell,
Then lifted on a crossing wind, alarm
The river parish by her mother's farm—
There, hearing how she'd come to little good,
She took a husband to dispirit hell."

She thinks of how she watched her husband drive
To meetings with Macaulay's life of Clive
Tucked in a pocket—there, unshaven, white,
And mumbling to himself, he would recite
The verses on Lucretia from the *Lay
Of Ancient Rome,* and ape her Roman way
Of falling from dishonor on a sword;
And yet she'd thought her kindness had restored
Pearl Harbor's shell-shock, thought he would enjoy . . .
As if God's touch, as if Jehovah's joy,
Allowed him to resume the wearisome
Renown of merely living, when he'd come,
Like Atlas with the world about his ears,
To tell her nothing. Once again she hears
Her husband's stubborn laugh. A pair of boulder
Gray squirrels romp like kittens on his shoulder.

Then it was Christmas. "Harry's mine for good,"
She'd shouted, running down the stairs to find
Him stumbling for his little strip of wood
To stir the bowl. She sees the flurries blind
The barren Christmas greens, as winter dusks
The double window, and she hears the slow
Treck of the Magi hoofing cotton snow
Behind their snow-shoes on the golden husks
Of birdseed cast like breadcrumbs for their three
Gold-dusty camels by the Christmas tree,
A withered creeping hemlock in a cup;
Its star of hope and only ornament,
A silver dollar. He turned the burners up,
And stirred the stoup of glüg—a quart of grain,
Two quarts of claret, every condiment,
Berry and nut and rind and herb in Maine!

"You went to bed, Love, finished—through, through, through.
Hoping to find you useless, dead asleep,
I stole to bed beside you, after two
As usual. Had you drugged yourself to keep
Your peace? I think so. If our bodies met,
You'd flinch, and flounder on your face. I heard
The snowplow banging; its eye-headlights set
On mine—a clowning dragon—so absurd,
Its thirty gangling feet of angled lights,
Red, blue and orange. Having broken loose
From Ringling Brothers, it had lost the use
Of sense, Love, and was worming days and nights
To hole up *some*where. Then I slept. I found
That I was stalking in my moccasins
Below the mill-fall, where our cave begins
To shake its head, a green Medusa, crowned

With juniper. A dragon writhed around
A knob above you, and its triple tails
Fanned at your face. Furlongs of glaucous scales
Wallowed to splatter the reproachful hound
Eyes of the gorgon on the monstrous targe,
Plated with hammered-down tobacco tins,
You pushed and parried at the water's charge.
Your blue and orange broadsword lopped its fins
And roaring . . . I was back in bed. The day
Was graying on us. So that you could keep
An eye upon them, Harry, sword and shield
Loomed from your shoebag. "I will have to yield
You to the dragon, if you fall asleep."
You pulled my nightgown. "Maiden, they have belled
The dragon's tail. The dragon's on its way
To woo you." Then I slept. Your fingers held. . . .

"You *held* me! 'Please, Love, let your elbows . . . quick,
Quick it!' I shook you, 'can't you see how sick
This playing . . . take me; Harry's driving back.
Take me!' 'Who am I?' 'You are you; not black
Like Harry; you're a boy. Look out, his car's
White eyes are at the window. Boy, your chin
Is bristling. You have gored me black and blue.
I am all prickle-tickle like the stars;
I am a sleepy-foot, a dogfish skin
Rubbed backwards, wrongways; you have made my hide
Split snakey, Bad one—*one!*' Then I was wide
Awake, and turning over. 'Who, who, who?'
You asked me, 'tell me who.' Then everything
Was roaring, Harry. Harry, I could feel
Nothing—it was so black—except your seal,
The stump with green shoots on your signet ring.

92

"I couldn't tell you; but you shook the bed,
And struck me, Harry. 'I will shake you dead
As earth,' you chattered, 'you, you, you, you, you. . . .
Who are you keeping, Anne?' you mocked me, 'Anne,
You want yourself.' I gagged, and then I ran.
My maid was knocking. Snow was chasing through
The open window. 'Harry, I am glad
You tried to kill me; it is out, you know;
I'll shout it from the housetops of the Mills;
I'll tell you, so remember, you are mad;
I'll tell them, listen Harry: husband kills
His wife for dreaming. You must help. No, no!
I've always loved you; I am just a girl;
You mustn't choke me!' Then I thought the beams
Were falling on us. Things began to whirl.
'Harry, we're not accountable for dreams.'

"Spread-eagled backward on your backless chair,
Inhaling the regardless, whirling air,
Rustling about you from the oven jets,
Sparkling and crackling on the cigarettes
Still burning in the saucer, where you'd tossed
Almost a carton, Love, before you lost
All sense of caring, and I saw your eyes
Looking in wonder at your bloody hand—
And like an angler wading out from land,
Who feels the bottom shelving, while he sees
His nibbled bobber twitch the dragonflies:
You watched your hand withdrawing by degrees—
Enthralled and fearful—till it stopped beneath
Your collar, and you felt your being drip
Blue-purple with a joy that made your teeth
Grin all to-whichways through your lower lip.

"I must have fainted. Harry, where I sank,
The gulls were yelping and a river stank,
And I was seated in a wicker chair
Beside a tub of crabs. And you were there
Above me and I held a jelly-roll
And read the comics, while you stood to pole
Our dory with a pitchfork to the pier.
You shout directions, but I cannot steer
Because the boat stops, and the spilling tub
Bubbles with torment, as you trip and lance
Your finger at a crab. It strikes. You rub
It inch-meal to a bilge of shell. You dance
Child-crazy over tub and gunnel, grasping
Your pitchfork like a trident, poised to stab
The greasy eel-grass clasping and unclasping
The jellied iridescence of the crab.

"Then yellow water, and the summer's drought
Boiled on its surface underneath our grounds'
Disordered towzle. *Wish my, wish my, wish,*
Said the dry-flies snapping past my ears to whip
Those dead-horse waters, faster than a fish
Could follow—longer too. I gasped. My mouth
Was open, and I seemed to mime your hound's
Terrified panting; and our trimming ship
Was shipping water . . . I was staring at
Our drifting oars. The moon was floating—flat
As the old world of maps. I thought, 'I'll stay.
Harry,' I whispered, 'hurry, I will pray
So truly; hurry! God, you must, you must
Hurry, for Death, carousing like a king
On nothing but his lands, will take your ring
To bind me, and possess me to the dust.'

94

"Then life went on; you lived, or lived at least
To baby-smile into the brutal gray
Daylight each morning, and your sofa lay
Beside the window, and you watched the east
Wind romping, till it swept the sullen blue
Bluster of April in the mouth of May,
The month of mating. Yellow warblers flew
About the ivied window, calling you.
You smiled. Then your eyes wandered to alight
As aliens on your charts of black and white
New England birds: the kinds, once memorized
By number, now no longer recognized,
Were numbers, numbers! 'What's the twenty-eight,
The twenty-eight, the twenty-eight—O wait:
A cardinal bird, a scarlet tanager,
The redbird that I used to whittle her.'

"You lived. Your rocker creaked, as you declined.
To the ungarnished ruin of your mind
Came the persona of the murderous Saul
In dirty armor, followed by a boy,
Who twanged a jew's-harp. Stumbling on one leg,
You speared our quaking shadows to the wall.
'Where is my harper? Music! Must I beg
For music?' Then you sucked your thumb for joy,
And baby-smiled through strings of orange juice.
'Where are you, Anne? A harper for the King.'
When the phantasmagoria left, you wept
For their return. Ah Harry, what's the use
Of lying? I called the doctor while you slept.
'Now it's as if he'd never lived,' I thought;
'As if I'd never, never anything.'
I felt the stump and green shoots at my throat.

" 'Sleep, sleep,' I hushed you. 'Sleep. You must abide
The lamentations of the nuptial mass—
Then you are rising. Then you are alive;
The bridesmaids scatter daisies, and the bride,
A daisy choired by daisies, sings: "My life
Is like a horn of plenty gone to grass,
Or like the yellow bee-queen in her hive."
She whispers, "Who is this, and who is this?
His eyes are coals. His breath is myrrh; his kiss,
The consummation of the silvered glass.
His lightning slivers through me like a knife." '
The door is open, but I hope to pass
Unheard. Your male-attendant tries to feed
You. I can hear him talking (O for keeps!)
'Mother of Jesus, had her while she sleeps;
She took him for the other guy, she'd . . .' *She'd!*"

Then summer followed: children rollerskate
And fight with hockey sticks about a crate
Of cannon crackers. They have mined the road.
Someone is shouting. Tufts of grass explode.
Somewhere a child is dancing in his grease
And war-paint. "Mees," he shouts, "town ring! Mees, Mees,
Town ring. Lieutenant Kavanaugh eeth dead."
She sees the body sitting up in bed
Before the window. "You must bury me
As if you gloried in my liberty.
I died," it seems to tell her, "while July,
The month of freedom, tigerstriped the sky
With bombs and rockets." How will she disown
The leisured condescension of his frown
That still refuses, while she moves about
The body, saying, "Blow the candle out."

"But it's so dull," she whispers, "it's so dull,
This autumn, Harry, from the line-storm lull
Through Hallows', playing Patience to defeat
Poor *Sol*. Pearl Harbor's whole Pacific fleet
Has sea-room in my mind. Here, Peace, the Pearl
Hawaiians dive for . . . I am just a girl,
Just one man's not the fleet's." She stands, then sits
And makes a card-house; it's as if her wits
Were overseas. The cards are Kavanaughs,
Or sinister, bewildered effigies
Of kings and queens. Another game begins;
Shuffling so badly that she always wins,
She dreams her luck has brought her husband home.
"Harry," she whispers, "listen, the applause
Is rising for you. Gods of ancient Rome
Rise from the mill-pond on their marble knees.

"They watch like water-polo players—their eyes,
Stars of a recognition, no disguise
Or veil will hinder, now that they have found
Me their Persephone, gone underground
Into myself to supplicate the throne
And horn of Hades to restore that stone,
Imperial garland, once the living flower,
Now stone—Harvest, my mother's, only dower
To the dark monarch, and the futile dead
In Hades, where I lost my maidenhead.
Horns of the moon, they chant, *our Goddess.*" Then
She wakes. She stacks her cards, and once again
She rambles down the weedy path, past hill
And graveyard to the ruined burlap mill.
She lifts a pail. She pushes on an oar.
Her metal boat is moving from the shore.

The heron warps its neck, a broken pick,
To study its reflection on the scales,
Or knife-bright shards of water lilies, quick
In the dead autumn water with their snails
And water lice. Her ballet glasses hold
Him twisted by a fist of spruce, as dry
As flint and steel. She thinks: "The bird is old,
A cousin to all scholars; that is why
He will abet my thoughts of Kavanaugh,
Who gave the Mills its lumberyard and weir
In eighteen hundred, when our farmers saw
John Adams bring their Romish church a bell,
Cast—so the records claim—by Paul Revere.
The sticks of *Kavanaugh* are buried here—
Many of them, too many, Love, to tell—
Faithful to where their virgin forest fell.

And now the mussed blue-bottles bead her float:
Bringers of luck. Of luck? At worst, a rest
From counting blisters on her metal boat,
That spins and staggers. North and south and west:
A scene, perhaps, of Fragonard—her park,
Whose planted poplars scatter penny-leaves,
White underneath, like mussels to the dark
Chop of the shallows. Extirpation grieves
The sunken martyred laughter of the loon,
Where Harry's mother bathed in navy-blue
Stockings and skirts. But now, the afternoon
Is sullen, it is all that she can do
To lift the anchor. She can hardly row
Against these whitecaps—surely never lulled
For man and woman. Washing to and fro,
The floorboards bruise the lilies that she pulled.

"Even in August it was autumn—all
A pond could harbor." Now her matches fall
In dozens by her bobber to expire
As target-circles on the mirrored fire-
Escapes of *Kavanaugh*. She sees they hold
Her mirror to her—just a little cold;
A ground hog's looking glass. "The day is sharp
And short, Love, and its sun is like this carp,
Or goldfish, almost twenty inches long,
Panting, a weak old dog, below a prong
Of deadwood fallen from my copper beech;
The settling leaves embower its warmth. They reach
For my reflection, but it glides through shoal
Aground, to where the squirrel held its roots
And freehold, Love, unsliding, when our boots
Pattered—a life ago once—on its hole.

"I think we row together, for the stern
Jumps from my weaker stroke, and down the cove
Our house is floating, and the windows burn,
As if its underpinnings fed the stove.
Her window's open; look, she waits for us,
And types, until the clattering tin bell
Upon her room-large table tolls for us.
Listen, your mother's asking, *is it well?*
Yes, very well. He died outside the church
Like Harry Tudor. Now we near the sluice
And burial ground above the burlap mill;
I see you swing a string of yellow perch
About your head to fan off gnats that mill
And wail, as your disheartened shadow tries
The buried bedstead, where your body lies—
Time out of mind—a failing stand of spruce.

"God knows!" she marvels. "Harry, *Kavanaugh*
Was lightly given. Soon enough we saw
Death like the Bourbon after Waterloo,
Who learning and forgetting nothing, knew
Nothing but ruin. Why must we mistrust
Ourselves with Death who takes the world on trust?
Although God's brother, and himself a god,
Death whipped his horses through the startled sod;
For neither conscience nor omniscience warned
Him from his folly, when the virgin scorned
His courtship, and the quaking earth revealed
Death's desperation to the Thracian field.
And yet we think the virgin took no harm:
She gave herself because her blood was warm—
And for no other reason, Love, I gave
Whatever brought me gladness to the grave."

Falling Asleep over the Aeneid

An old man in Concord forgets to go to morning service. He falls asleep, while reading Vergil, and dreams that he is Aeneas at the funeral of Pallas, an Italian prince.

THE sun is blue and scarlet on my page,
And *yuck-a, yuck-a, yuck-a, yuck-a,* rage
The yellowhammers mating. Yellow fire
Blankets the captives dancing on their pyre,
And the scorched lictor screams and drops his rod.
Trojans are singing to their drunken God,
Ares. Their helmets catch on fire. Their files
Clank by the body of my comrade—miles
Of filings! Now the scythe-wheeled chariot rolls
Before their lances long as vaulting poles,
And I stand up and heil the thousand men,
Who carry Pallas to the bird-priest. Then
The bird-priest groans, and as his birds foretold,
I greet the body, lip to lip. I hold
The sword that Dido used. It tries to speak,
A bird with Dido's sworded breast. Its beak
Clangs and ejaculates the Punic word
I hear the bird-priest chirping like a bird.
I groan a little. "Who am I, and why?"
It asks, a boy's face, though its arrow-eye
Is working from its socket. "Brother, try,
O Child of Aphrodite, try to die:
To die is life." His harlots hang his bed
With feathers of his long-tailed birds. His head
Is yawning like a person. The plumes blow;
The beard and eyebrows ruffle. Face of snow,
You are the flower that country girls have caught,

A wild bee-pillaged honey-suckle brought
To the returning bridegroom—the design
Has not yet left it, and the petals shine;
The earth, its mother, has, at last, no help:
It is itself. The broken-winded yelp
Of my Phoenician hounds, that fills the brush
With snapping twigs and flying, cannot flush
The ghost of Pallas. But I take his pall,
Stiff with its gold and purple, and recall
How Dido hugged it to her, while she toiled,
Laughing—her golden threads, a serpent coiled
In cypress. Now I lay it like a sheet;
It clinks and settles down upon his feet,
The careless yellow hair that seemed to burn
Beforehand. Left foot, right foot—as they turn,
More pyres are rising: armored horses, bronze,
And gagged Italians, who must file by ones
Across the bitter river, when my thumb
Tightens into their wind-pipes. The beaks drum;
Their headman's cow-horned death's-head bites its tongue,
And stiffens, as it eyes the hero slung
Inside his feathered hammock on the crossed
Staves of the eagles that we winged. Our cost
Is nothing to the lovers, whoring Mars
And Venus, father's lover. Now his car's
Plumage is ready, and my marshals fetch
His squire, Acoetes, white with age, to hitch
Aethon, the hero's charger, and its ears
Prick, and it steps and steps, and stately tears
Lather its teeth; and then the harlots bring
The hero's charms and baton—but the King,
Vain-glorious Turnus, carried off the rest.
"I was myself, but Ares thought it best

The way it happened." At the end of time,
He sets his spear, as my descendants climb
The knees of Father Time, his beard of scalps,
His scythe, the arc of steel that crowns the Alps.
The elephants of Carthage hold those snows,
Turms of Numidian horse unsling their bows,
The flaming turkey-feathered arrows swarm
Beyond the Alps. "Pallas," I raise my arm
And shout, "Brother, eternal health. Farewell
Forever." Church is over, and its bell
Frightens the yellowhammers, as I wake
And watch the whitecaps wrinkle up the lake.
Mother's great-aunt, who died when I was eight,
Stands by our parlor sabre. "Boy, it's late.
Vergil must keep the Sabbath." Eighty years!
It all comes back. My Uncle Charles appears.
Blue-capped and bird-like. Phillips Brooks and Grant
Are frowning at his coffin, and my aunt,
Hearing his colored volunteers parade
Through Concord, laughs, and tells her English maid
To clip his yellow nostril hairs, and fold
His colors on him. . . . It is I. I hold
His sword to keep from falling, for the dust
On the stuffed birds is breathless, for the bust
Of young Augustus weighs on Vergil's shelf:
It scowls into my glasses at itself.

Her Dead Brother

THE Lion of St. Mark's upon the glass
Shield in my window reddens, as the night
Enchants the swinging dories to its terrors,
And dulls your distant wind-stung eyes; alas,
Your portrait, coiled in German-silver hawsers, mirrors
The sunset as a dragon. Enough light
Remains to see you through your varnish. Giving
Your life has brought you closer to your friends;
Yes, it has brought you home. All's well that ends:
Achilles dead is greater than the living;

My mind holds you as I would have you live,
A wintering dragon. Summer was too short
When we went picnicking with telescopes
And crocking leather handbooks to that fort
Above the lank and heroned Sheepscot, where its slopes
Are clutched by hemlocks—spotting birds. I give
You back that idyll, Brother. Was it more?
Remember riding, scotching with your spur
That four-foot milk-snake in a juniper?
Father shellacked it to the ice-house door.

Then you were grown; I left you on your own.
We will forget that August twenty-third,
When Mother motored with the maids to Stowe,
And the pale summer shades were drawn—so low
No one could see us; no, nor catch your hissing word,
As false as Cressid! Let our deaths atone:
The fingers on your sword-knot are alive,
And Hope, that fouls my brightness with its grace,
Will anchor in the narrows of your face.
My husband's Packard crunches up the drive.

The ice is out: the tidal current swims
Its blocks against the launches as they pitch
Under the cruisers of my Brother's fleet.
The gas, uncoiling from my oven burners, dims
The face above this bottled *Water Witch,*
The knockabout my Brother fouled and left to eat
Its heart out by the Boston Light. My Brother,
I've saved you in the ice-house of my mind—
The ice is out. . . . Our fingers lock behind
The tiller. We are heeling in the smother,

Our sails, balloon and leg-o'mutton, tell
The colors of the rainbow; but they flap,
As the wind fails, and cannot fetch the bell. . . .
His stick is tapping on the millwheel-step,
He lights a match, another and another—
The Lord is dark, and holy is His name;
By my own hands, into His hands! My burners
Sing like a kettle, and its nickel mirrors
Your squadron by the Stygian Landing. Brother,
The harbor! The torpedoed cruisers flame,

The motor-launches with their searchlights bristle
About the targets. You are black. You shout,
And cup your broken sword-hand. Yes, your whistle
Across the crackling water: *Quick, the ice is out.* . . .
The wind dies in our canvas; we were running dead
Before the wind, but now our sail is part
Of death. O Brother, a New England town is death
And incest—and I saw it whole. I said,
Life is a thing I own. Brother, my heart
Races for sea-room—we are out of breath.

Mother Marie Therese

DROWNED IN 1912

Old sisters at our Maris Stella House
Remember how the Mother's strangled grouse
And snow-shoe rabbits matched the royal glint
Of Pio Nono's vestments in the print
That used to face us, while our aching ring
Of stationary rockets saw her bring
Our cake. Often, when sunset hurt the rocks
Off Carthage, and surprised us knitting socks
For victims of the Franco-Prussian War,
Our scandal'd set her frowning at the floor;
And vespers struck like lightning through the gloom
And oaken ennui of her sitting room.
It strikes us now, but cannot re-inspire;
False, false and false, I mutter to my fire.
The good old times, ah yes! But good, that all's
Forgotten like our Province's cabals;
And Jesus, smiling earthward, finds it good;
For we were friends of Cato, not of God.
This sixtieth Christmas, I'm content to pray
For what life's shrinkage leaves from day to day;
And it's a sorrow to recall our young
Raptures for Mother, when her trophies hung,
Fresh in their blood and color, to convince
Even Probationers that Heaven's Prince,
Befriending, whispered: "Is it then so hard?
Tarry a little while, O disregard
Time's wings and armor, when it flutters down
Papal tiaras and the Bourbon crown;
For quickly, priest and prince will stand, their shields

Before each other's faces, in the fields,
Where, as I promised, virtue will compel
Michael and all his angels to repel
Satan's advances, till his forces lie
Beside the Lamb in blissful fealty."
Our Indian summer! Then, our skies could lift,
God willing; but an Indian brought the gift.
"A sword," said Father Turbot, "not a saint";
Yet He who made the Virgin without taint,
Chastised our Mother to the Rule's restraint.
Was it not fated that the sweat of Christ
Would wash the worldly serpent? Christ enticed
Her heart that fluttered, while she whipped her hounds
Into the quicksands of her manor grounds,
A lordly child, her habit fleur-de-lys'd—
There she dismounted, sick; with little heed,
Surrendered. Like Proserpina, who fell
Six months a year from earth to flower in hell;
She half-renounced by Candle, Book and Bell
Her flowers and fowling pieces for the Church.
She never spared the child and spoiled the birch;
And how she'd chide her novices, and pluck
Them by the ears for gabbling in Canuck,
While she was reading Rabelais from her chaise,
Or parroting the *Action Française*.
Her letter from the soi-disant French King,
And the less treasured golden wedding ring
Of her shy Bridegroom, yellow; and the regal
Damascus shot-guns, pegged upon her eagle
Emblems from Hohenzollern standards, rust.
Our world is passing; even she, whose trust
Was in its princes, fed the gluttonous gulls,
That whiten our Atlantic, when like skulls
They drift for sewage with the emerald tide.

Perpetual novenas cannot tide
Us past that drowning. After Mother died,
"An émigrée in this world and the next,"
Said Father Turbot, playing with his text.
Where is he? Surely, he is one of those,
Whom Christ and Satan spew! But no one knows
What's happened to that porpoise-bellied priest.
He lodged with us on Louis Neuvième's Feast,
And celebrated her memorial mass.
His bald spot tapestried by colored glass,
Our angels, Prussian blue and flaking red,
He squeaked and stuttered: "N-n-nothing is so d-dead
As a dead s-s-sister." Off Saint Denis' Head,
Our Mother, drowned on an excursion, sleeps.
Her billy goat, or its descendant, keeps
Watch on a headland, and I hear it bawl
Into this sixty-knot Atlantic squall,
"Mamamma's Baby," past Queen Mary's Neck,
The ledge at Carthage—almost to Quebec,
Where Monsieur de Montcalm, on Abraham's
Bosom, asleep, perceives our world that shams
His New World, lost—however it atones
For Wolfe, the Englishman, and Huron bones
And priests'. O Mother, here our snuffling crones
And cretins feared you, but I owe you flowers:
The dead, the sea's dead, has her sorrows, hours
On end to lie tossing to the east, cold,
Without bed-fellows, washed and bored and old,
Bilged by her thoughts, and worked on by the worms,
Until her fossil convent come to terms
With the Atlantic. Mother, there is room
Beyond our harbor. Past its wooden Boom
Now weak and waterlogged, that Frontenac

Once diagrammed, she welters on her back.
The bell-buoy, whom she called the Cardinal,
Dances upon her. If she hears at all,
She only hears it tolling to this shore,
Where our frost-bitten sisters know the roar
Of water, inching, always on the move
For virgins, when they wish the times were love,
And their hysterical hosannahs rouse
The loveless harems of the buck ruffed grouse,
Who drums, untroubled now, beside the sea—
As if he found our stern virginity
Contra naturam. We are ruinous;
God's Providence through time has mastered us:
Now all the bells are tongueless, now we freeze,
A later Advent, pruner of warped trees,
Whistles about our nunnery slabs, and yells,
And water oozes from us into wells;
A new year swells and stirs. Our narrow Bay
Freezes itself and us. We cannot say
Christ even sees us, when the ice floes toss
His statue, made by Hurons, on the cross,
That Father Turbot sank on Mother's mound—
A whirligig! Mother, we must give ground,
Little by little; but it does no good.
Tonight, while I am piling on more driftwood,
And stooping with the poker, you are here,
Telling your beads; and breathing in my ear,
You watch your orphan swording at her fears.
I feel you twitch my shoulder. No one hears
Us mock the sisters, as we used to, years
And years behind us, when we heard the spheres
Whirring *venite;* and we held our ears.
My mother's hollow sockets fill with tears.

David and Bathsheba in the Public Garden

I

DAVID TO BATHSHEBA

"Worn out of virtue, as the time of year,
The burning City and its bells surround
The Public Garden. What is sound
Past agony is fall:
The children crowding home from school at five,
Punting a football in the bricky air—
You mourn Uriah? If he were alive,
O Love, my age were nothing but the ball
Of leaves inside this lion-fountain, left
For witch and winter." "Yet the leaves' complaint
Is the King's fall . . . whatever suffers theft."
"The Latin labels on the foreign trees are quaint.

The trees, for decades, shook their discontent
On strangers; rustling, rustling the Levant."
"Uriah might have found the want
Of what was never his
A moment, found the falling colors welcome."
"But he was dead before Jehovah sent
Our shadows to the lion's cave. What's come
Is dancing like a leaf for nothing. Kiss:
The leaves are dark and harp." "My Lord, observe
The shedding, park-bound mallards, how they keep
Circling and driving for Uriah's sleep;
Driven, derided, David, and my will a curve.

The fountain's falling waters ring around
The garden." "Love, if you had stayed my hand
Uriah would not understand
The lion's rush, or why
This stone-mouthed fountain laps us like a cat."
"And he is nothing after death but ground,
Anger and anguish, David? When we sat
The nights of summer out, the gravity
Of reaching for the moon. . . . Perhaps it took
Of fall, the Fall?" "Perhaps, I live. I lie
Drinking our likeness from the water. Look:
The Lion's mane and age! Surely, I will not die."

II

BATHSHEBA'S LAMENT IN THE GARDEN

Baring the mares'-nests that the squirrels set
To tangle with the wood-winds of the North,
October blows to wood . . . the fourth
Since David broke our vows
And married Abishag to warm him. Cold!
The pigeons bluer with it, since we met
Beside the lion-fountain, and unrolled
The tackle of our model boats. Our prows
Were sworded as the marlin, and they locked,
Clearing the mallards' grotto, half a mile
Up pond—and foundered; and our splashing mocked
The lion's wrinkled brow. My Love, a little while,

The lion frothed into the basin . . . all,
Water to water—water that begets
A child from water. And the jets
That washed our bodies drowned
The curses of Uriah when he died
For David; still a stranger! *Not-at-all,*
We called him, after the withdrawing tide
Of Joab's armor-bearers slew him, and he found
Jehovah, the whale's belly of the pit.
He is the childless, the unreconciled
Master of darkness. Will Uriah sit
And judge? You nod and babble. But, you are a child;

At last, a child—what we were playing, when
We blew our bubbles at the moon, and fought
Like brothers, and the lion caught
The moonbeams in its jaws.
The harvest moon, earth's friend, that cared so much
For us and cared so little, comes again;
Always a stranger! Farther from my touch,
The mountains of the moon . . . whatever claws
The harp-strings chalks the harper's fingers. Cold
The eyelid drooping on the lion's eye
Of David, child of fortune. I am old;
God is ungirded; open! I must surely die.

The Fat Man in the Mirror

[AFTER WERFEL]

WHAT's filling up the mirror? O, it is not I;
Hair-belly like a beaver's house? An old dog's eye?
    The forenoon was blue
    In the mad King's zoo
Nurse was swinging me so high, so high!

The bullies wrestled on the royal bowling green;
Hammers and sickles on their hoods of black sateen. . . .
    Sulking on my swing
    The tobacco King
Sliced apples with a pen-knife for the Queen.

This *I,* who used to mouse about the paraffined preserves,
And jammed a finger in the coffee-grinder, serves
    Time before the mirror.
    But this pursey terror . . .
Nurse, it is a person. *It is nerves.*

Where's the Queen-Mother waltzing like a top to staunch
The blood of Lewis, King of Faerie? Hip and haunch
    Lard the royal grotto;
    Straddling Lewis' motto,
Time, the Turk, its sickle on its paunch.

Nurse, Nurse, it rises on me . . . O, it starts to roll,
My apples, O, are ashes in the meerschaum bowl. . . .
    If you'd only come,
    If you'd only come,
Darling, if . . . The apples that I stole,

While Nurse and I were swinging in the Old One's eye . . .
Only a fat man with his beaver on his eye
Only a fat man,
Only a fat man
Bursts the mirror. O, it is not I!

Thanksgiving's Over

Thanksgiving night, 1942: a room on Third Avenue. Michael dreams of his wife, a German-American Catholic, who leapt from a window before she died in a sanatorium. The church referred to in the first and last stanzas is the Franciscan church on 31st Street.

THANKSGIVING night: Third Avenue was dead;
My fowl was soupbones. Fathoms overhead,
Snow warred on the El's world in the blank snow.
"Michael," she whispered, "just a year ago,
Even the shoreleave from the *Normandie*
Were weary of Thanksgiving; but they'd stop
And lift their hats. I watched their arctics drop
Below the birdstoup of the Anthony
And Child who guarded our sodality
For lay-Franciscans, Michael, till I heard
The birds inside me, and I knew the Third
Person possessed me, for I was the bird
Of Paradise, the parrot whose absurd
Garblings are glory. *Cherry ripe, ripe, ripe:*
I shrilled to Christ the Sailor's silver pipe
And cherry-tasselled tam. Now Michael sleeps,
Thanksgiving's over, nothing is for keeps:
New earth, new sky, new life: I hear the word
Of Brother Francis, child and bird, descend,
Calling the war of Michael a pretend;
The Lord is Brother Parrot, and a friend."

"Whose friend?" I answered. I was dreaming. Cars
Trampled the Elevated's scaffolding,
And jerked the fire-proofed pumpkins on the line
Her Aunt had fixed with Christophers and stars
To make her joyful; and the bars

Still caged her window—half a foot from mine,
It mirrored mine:
My window's window. On its cushioned ring,
Her celluloid and bargain cockatoo,
Yellow and blue,
Grew restive from her fingering—
Poor numskull, he had beebees in his tail.
"The birds inside me choir to Christ the Healer;
Thanksgiving's over." She was laughing. Bars
Shielded her vigil-candle, while it burned
Pin-beaded, indigo:
A bluebird in a tumbler. "Let me go!
Michael," she whispered, "all I want to do
Is kill you." Then the bars
Crashed with her, and I saw her vanishing
Into the neon of the restaurant—
Clawing and screaming . . . "If you're worth the burying
And burning, Michael, God will let you know
Your merits for the love I felt the want
Of, when your mercy shipped me to Vermont

To the asylum. Michael, was there warrant
For killing love? As if the birds that range
The bestiary-garden by my cell,
Like angels in the needle-point, my Aunt
Bequeathed our altar guild, could want
To hurt a fly! . . . But Michael, I was well;
My mind was well;
I wanted to be loved—to thaw, to change,
To *April!* Now our mountains, seventeen
Bald Brothers, green
Below the timberline, must change
Their skullcaps for the green of Sherwood Forest;
Mount Leather-Jacket leads the season. Outlaws,

We enter a world of children, perched on gaunt
Crows-nests in hemlocks over flat-iron torrents;
And freely serve our term
In prison. I will serve you, Love. Affirm
The promise, move the mountains, while they lean,
As dry as dust for want
Of trusting. Michael, look, the lordly range
Over our brooks' chorale of broken rocks,
Lifting a bowshot's distance, clouds and suffers change—
Blue cloud! There, ruin toils not, though infirm:
Our water-shed! Our golden weathercocks
Are creaking: Fall is here, and starlings. Flocks
Scavenge for El Dorado in the hemlocks.

O Michael, hurry up and ring my bell.
Ring, ring for me! . . . Why do you make us kneel?
Why are we praying? Michael, Venus locks
My lattice, lest a chatterbox
Archangel—O so jealous—spoil and steal
Her commonweal,
My bedroom. Is it just another cell,
This *primavera,* where the Graces wear
Only the air:
Unmarried April! It is hell!
A lying-in house where the Virtues wither.
I promise, Michael. Michael, I will promise.
I promise on my kneeler—in these stocks!
Your Virtues, owls or parrots, bend my ear
And babble: *Chatterer,*
Our owlet, once in a blue moon we stir;
Our elbows almost touch you. How we care
And worry, Goldielocks;
Thanksgiving's Goose, poor loveless Venus: life's a sell:
Our loveless fingers crook to crunch your sage

And parsley through your wishbone—you! I'll tell
You, Michael Darling: an adulterer,
My Husband, shows me in a parrot's cage
And feeds me like a lion. While I age,

Virtues and elders eye me. Love, the outrage
Would have undone me, if my mind had held
Together, half a moment. Altar boys
Lit candles with my diary. Page by page,
Its refuse, sparkling through my cage,
Branded me, Michael!" Then a popping noise:
It was her toy's
Fragments: her cockatoo. She yelled.
The whisky tumbler in her hand
Became a brand.
Her pigtails that her Aunt had belled
To tell us she was coming, flashed and tinkled.
"Husband, you used to call me Tomcat-kitten;
While we were playing Hamlet on our stage
With curtain rods for foils, my eyes were bleeding;
I was your valentine.
You are a bastard, Michael, aren't you! *Nein,*
Michael. It's no more valentines." Her hand
Covered her eyes to cage
Their burning from the daylight. Sleep dispelled
The burden of her spirit. But the cars
Rattled my window. *Where am I to go?* She yelled:
"Let go my apron!" And I saw them shine,
Her eyeballs—like a lion at the bars
Across my open window—like the stars!

Winter had come on horseback, and the snow,
Hostile and unattended, wrapped my feet
In sheepskins. Where I'd stumbled from the street,

A red cement Saint Francis fed a row
Of toga'd boys with birds beneath a Child.
His candles flamed in tumblers, and He smiled.
"Romans!" she whispered, "look, these overblown
And bootless Brothers tell us we must go
Barefooted through the snow where birds recite:
Come unto us, our burden's light—light, light,
This burden that our marriage turned to stone!
O Michael, must we join this deaf and dumb
Breadline for children? Sit and listen." So
I sat. I counted to ten thousand, wound
My cowhorn beads from Dublin on my thumb,
And ground them. *Miserere?* Not a sound.